Voting Hopes or Fears?

◆   ◆   ◆   ◆   ◆

Voting Hopes
or
Fears?

◆   ◆   ◆   ◆   ◆

White Voters,
Black Candidates
& Racial Politics
in America

KEITH REEVES

New York   Oxford   ◆   Oxford University Press   1997

Oxford University Press

Oxford   New York
Athens   Auckland   Bangkok   Bogota   Bombay
Buenos Aires   Calcutta   Cape Town   Dar es Salaam
Delhi   Florence   Hong Kong   Istanbul   Karachi
Kuala Lumpur   Madras   Madrid   Melbourne
Mexico City   Nairobi   Paris   Singapore
Taipei   Tokyo   Toronto   Warsaw

and associated companies in
Berlin   Ibadan

Copyright ©1997 by Keith Reeves

Published by Oxford University Press, Inc.
198 Madison Avenue, New York, New York 10016

Oxford is a registered trademark of Oxford University Press

Library of Congress Cataloging-in-Publication Data
Reeves, Keith.
Voting hopes or fears?: white voters, black candidates, and racial politics
in America/Keith Reeves
p.   cm.
Includes bibliographical references and index.
ISBN 0-19-510161-8; ISBN 0-19-510162-6 (pbk.)
1. Voting—United States.   2. Elections—United States.
3. Race discrimination—Political aspects—United States.
4. Racism—Political aspects—United States.   I. Title.
JK1976.R44 1997
324.7'0973'09049—dc21   96-36850

135798642
Printed in the United States of America
on acid-free paper

For

DeLois M. and Edwin A. Collins,
Louise A. Jackson,
Lena L. Reeves, and
Richard L. Rubin,
for instilling in me the idea that
"not failure but low aim is sin."

Acknowledgments

◆ ◆ ◆

When I informed my family and friends that I was writing a book on the controversial subject of racial politics, both authors and nonauthors alike proffered the same prediction: I would immerse myself in a solitary, hermit-like existence for a *very* long period of time. With nearly two years of "purgatory" firmly behind me, I would amend their prediction of this challenging enterprise somewhat. It was—to my pleasant surprise—more collaborative than solitary. Indeed, I have been extraordinarily fortunate at every stage in the process to have had the generous support of numerous colleagues and friends.

I owe large and lasting debts then, to Richard L. Allen, Reynolds Farley, James H. Johnson Jr., Gregory Markus, Vincent Price, Richard L. Rubin, Charlotte Steeh, and Michael W. Traugott. Besides providing invaluable counsel, assistance, and relentless encouragement from the project's inception, each made powerful contributions in support of me personally. I trust that the book is a worthy testament to their investment.

In the category of particular acknowledgments must also be included close friends Nadine Cohodas, Cecil Hale, and again, both James Johnson and Richard Rubin. In addition to offering invaluable commentary on the entire manuscript, this remarkable group of individuals helped me produce a better book that I hope will make a broader contribution to a national conversation on race and politics; my undergraduate and graduate student research assistants—Kristin Bunce, Margaret Fortune, Lorna Gougis, Eric Jackson, Veronica Jung, and Yvonne Malloy—for going beyond the call of duty; and Mary Jane Rose, not only for her assistance in producing the countless tables, figures, and graphs, but also for teaching me so much about "politics." I have taken each and every lesson to heart.

Moreover, as I was preparing the book for publication, my colleague and friend, Leon Higginbotham invited me to serve as an expert witness in a suit challenging the drawing of Louisiana's Fourth congressional district. There are no adequate words to describe what an enriching experience it has been working and teaching with "The Judge," as he is affectionately known. As such, I owe a special debt to him for his professional and personal mentoring; for penning the book's foreword. And my appreciation to Colleen Adams, Debo P. Adegbile, Jacqueline Berrien, David A. Bositis, Gregory A. Clarick, Robert Richie, Scharn Robinson, Brenda Wright, and Linda Y. Yueh for their contributions as well.

I owe considerable gratitude to my colleagues and friends at the Joan Shorenstein Center on the Press, Politics and Public Policy at Harvard's John F. Kennedy School of Government: Robert J. Blendon, Julie Felt, Daniel Gitterman, Edie Holway, Maxine Isaacs, Michele Johnson, Marion Just, John Lee, Jonathan Moore, Pippa Norris, W. Russell Neuman, Nancy Palmer, Richard Parker, Thomas Patterson, Jennifer Quinlan, Fred Shauer, and notably Marvin Kalb, the Center's director. They provided such a stimulating environment within which a young social scientist interested in pursuing the intersection of race, politics, and public policy could study, listen, and learn.

This research could not have been conducted without the generous financial support of the following institutions: the political science program at the National Science Foundation (Grant SES-9016766), Fannie-Mae, the Ford Foundation, the Russell Sage Foundation, the Social Science Research Council, the Research Program on Media and Politics in the Center for Political Studies at the Institute for Social Research and the College of Literature, Science and Arts—both at the University of Michigan. I benefited also from generous research awards from the Dean's Research Fund of the Kennedy School and the Goldsmith Research Award Program administered by the Shorenstein Center. And, a note of appreciation to Alan A. Altshuler for his support and encouragement.

Special acknowledgments must be given to Gioia Stevens, Thomas LeBien, Nancy Hoagland, Jessica Ryan, and Jeffrey Soloway of Oxford University Press. Their enthusiasm for the project never waned or wavered. And, it was such a pleasure working with them to bring the book to publication.

Grateful acknowledgment is made for permission to reprint Reynolds Farley, Charlotte Steeh, Maria Krysan, Tara Jackson, and Keith Reeves, "Stereotypes and Segregation: Neighborhoods in the Detroit Area," *American Journal of Sociology,* volume 100, number 3 (November 1994): 750–780, copyright © 1994 by The University of Chicago Press.

Last and certainly not least, profound and abiding gratitude is expressed to my wife, colleague, and best friend, Tara Diane Jackson. Despite working on her own research, she found ample time and energy to listen to, debate, and critique the ideas I've attempted to articulate here. This book would have been a much less interesting and rigorous endeavor had it not been for her wise counsel and support. For this—and so much more—I remain indebted.

Contents

◆ ◆ ◆

Foreword

♦ ♦ ♦

Hatred that rages in souls and suddenly loses its immediate object does not disappear without a trace.

—Anonymous, 1991

The precept of black inferiority[1] is the hate that raged in the American soul through over 240 years of slavery and nearly ninety years of segregation. Once slavery was abolished, and once the more oppressive forms of segregation were eliminated, many whites' hate still had not lost its immediate impact. The ashes of that hate have, over the course of so many generations, accumulated at the bottom of our memory. There they lie uneasily, like a heavy secret that whites can never quite confess, and blacks can never quite forgive, and which, for both blacks and whites, forestalls until a distant day any hope of peace and redemption.[2]

There is no issue more wrenching than race in America. The issue of race resides in the deepest and more secretive place in the American soul. Our attitudes about race are not in the open to be thoughtfully examined, but lie within the mind. Similarly, the most devastating manifestation of those racial attitudes does not take place openly, but occurs behind the closed curtain of the voting booth. It is there that the racial animus that pervades our national consciousness perhaps realizes its most damaging potential—white voters who vote against black candidates based on race and black voters who vote against white candidates based on race. For decades, blacks have voted for white candidates, even when the whites were not as effective as they should be to assure fairness and racial equality; however, Professor Keith Reeves establishes that there is no equivalent reciprocity by white voters when blacks are office-seekers.

This central question of what happens when a black face turns away white voters and the related question of whether a black candidate can ever be elected from settings where whites comprise a majority of the voters are the essence of not only this magnificent book, but are the critical contentions of the volatile arena of racial politics in America today.

The recent Congressional redistricting cases, starting from the devastating decision[3] of the Supreme Court in 1993 in *Shaw v. Reno* to the recent decision of the federal district court in Louisiana to strike down a majority-minority district in *Hays* v. *Louisiana III*, have turned the Equal Protection Clause of the Fourteenth Amendment on its head. As President Lyndon B. Johnson stated when he signed the 1965 Voting Rights Act, this measure to enfranchise African-Americans stemmed from a "clear and simple wrong." Yet, with the decision in *Shaw*, the ability of African-Americans, who have been historically disenfranchised, to bring racial pluralism to Congress has been dramatically reduced. The rationale of the Voting Rights Act and its guarantee of equal opportunity has been replaced by a doctrine of color-blindness that, in practice, maintains the status quo of white dominance. As Justice White stated in a dissent in *Shaw*, this new doctrine that majority-minority districts violate the Fourteenth Amendment is "both a fiction and a departure from settled equal protection principles."[4]

Professor Reeves's book provides empirical evidence that opens the curtain to the voting booth and into the racial attitudes of white voters. He demonstrates through an innovative experimental study that racially polarized voting exists among white voters against black candidates, and that in electoral politics, one's chance of winning an election is most often dependent on one's race. This persuasive new data on racially polarized voting requires each of us to reconsider the necessity of corrective measures in the arena of public policy that is most strongly correlated with the fundamental rights of citizenship—voting. The existence of racially biased voting prevents black candidates from fairly and equally pursuing elected office, which is a critical part of being full and equal participants in civic life. The perhaps unintentional cue by the press about race coupled with the persistence of racially biased attitudes of white voters provide a strong case for the continuing need for remedial measures, such as majority-minority districts, to ensure that we are closer to the day when there will be a level playing field for every American.

It is this hopeful conviction that led me to litigate the congressional redistricting case as *pro bono publico* chief counsel for Congressman Cleo Fields of Louisiana in 1995.[5] Because I was sixty-eight years old, at times, even my family because of health reasons questioned the wisdom of my spending so much energy to oppose the political injustice that the plaintiffs sought to impose.[6] Because the stakes were so high, it also led Professor Reeves to spend his considerable energy and wisdom as a *pro bono publico* expert witness. His testimony and that of other experts was critical in establishing the continuing existence of racially polarized voting in America, so that our case could be made on data-based, legally cogent, and morally persuasive grounds.

Unfortunately, the results were disastrous for persons who sought significant racial pluralism in Congress. Now, rather than Louisiana having two African-American Representatives, the state probably will have only one African-American in Congress—William Jefferson from New Orleans. *Voting Hopes or Fears?* makes an important contribution to our understanding of voting behavior. I hope that it will make a cumulative impact on increasing our national understanding about race—and as to the formidable challenges our nation still faces.

This book should not be read as being only relevant to those who are avid followers of politics and elections or other sorts of policy wonks and pundits. This book opens the secret place in the American soul that we do not usually talk about—the reality that the issue of race still pervades our consciousness and can be detrimental to the very idea of democracy itself through its adverse impact on the ability of a minority group to exercise its fundamental rights of citizenship. It is the potential opening of the soul that should inspire every American to read this book. It is a controversial, daring, and honest description of racial politics in America today from an exciting new scholar, whose insights can teach us and whose name we will be hearing about for many decades to come.

—A. Leon Higginbotham Jr.
Chief Judge Emeritus, U.S. Court of Appeals and
Public Service Professor of Jurisprudence
John F. Kennedy School of Government, Harvard University

Voting Hopes or Fears?

Vote your hopes, not your fears.

—David Dinkins, 1989

There was an unfounded fear. . . . The idea that blacks once they take power will engage in retributive justice is just not so.

—Jesse Jackson on Harold Washington's mayoral win, 1983

Introduction

✦ ✦ ✦

The Voting Rights Act expressly provides that black . . . voters must be afforded an equal opportunity "to participate in the political process and to elect representatives of their choice."

—Lani Guinier, *The Tyranny of the Majority*

The United States has long cherished the belief that every individual has a "fair chance and an open road" to realize his or her dreams and aspirations. So it should come as no great surprise that there has been a dramatic sea change in the nation's thinking regarding affirmative action. Believing that racial discrimination is less pernicious today, an implacably hostile chorus of whites (and an increasing number of black Americans) contend that "preferential treatment," "set-asides," "quotas," or "entitlements" for any one categorical group is fundamentally unfair, counterproductive—if not divisive— and wholly antithetical to the principle of individual merit.

For instance, a 1995 *Newsweek* poll on whether qualified blacks should receive preferential treatment over equally qualified whites with regard to getting into college or getting jobs found that a striking 79 percent of the whites surveyed believe that qualified blacks should *not* be given such special consideration over equally qualified whites. In contrast, 46 percent of blacks concurred.[1] Figures from the 1994 National Election Studies conducted by the Center for Political Studies at the University of Michigan, point out that while four out of ten blacks believe the federal government has a responsibility to improve their position in society, only two in ten whites tend to agree.[2] Besides, an overwhelming majority of white Americans believe that blacks in fact have an equal chance to succeed in life.[3] Such a chasm in public opinion comes as no great surprise to any astute and thoughtful observer of American racial politics. These figures nevertheless typify the fundamentally contrasting perspectives held by black and white Americans regarding the federal government's approval of remedies to bring about parity between blacks and whites throughout the society.

Only three decades earlier, President Lyndon B. Johnson delivered what is still the most eloquent and justifiable argument on behalf of the federal government's stance on affirmative action.[4] Addressing a captive Howard University commencement audience on June 4, 1965, the president remarked:

> You do not wipe away the scars of centuries by saying: Now you are free to go where you want and do as you desire and choose the leaders you please. You do not take a person who, for years, has been hobbled by chains and liberate him, bring him to the starting line of a race, and then say you are free to compete with all the others, and still just believe that you have been completely fair. Thus it is not enough just to open the gates of opportunity. All our citizens must have the ability to walk through those gates. This is the next and the more profound state of the battle for civil rights. We seek not just freedom but opportunity. We seek not just legal equity but human ability, not just equality as a right and a theory but equality as a fact and equality as a result.[5]

Against the backdrop of the volatile and tenuous social climate of the 1960s, such a forceful, articulate, and unequivocal pronouncement from the lips of the southern Democratic president was both politically courageous and admittedly poignant. No one, not even the president of the United States, could deny that although it had already begun to dismantle the constitutionally sanctioned mores and customs that served as the linchpin of social segregation, the nation still had to contend with the vestiges of the ignominious legacy of racial prejudice and discrimination.

The president was also likely thinking of the impending struggle his administration would wage with Congress over federal legislation protecting the voting rights of black Americans. Only three months before, the nation watched in horror and disbelief as blacks—peacefully participating in a voting rights protest march from Selma to Montgomery—were brutally attacked by state troopers, deputy sheriffs, and volunteer officers. The events of "Bloody Sunday" would become the catalyst for an invigorated commitment on the part of the Johnson administration to secure comprehensive voting rights legislation guaranteeing the right to vote without regard to "race, color, or previous condition of servitude."

Perchance cognizant of the inherent hypocrisy between revered American ideals—liberty, equality, fairness, justice—and the nation's less than equitable treatment of its black citizens, the president's comments at Howard University suggest that he was moving beyond mere lip service to what the Swedish-born sociologist Gunnar Myrdal termed "the American Creed." Writing in his monumental study, *An American Dilemma: The Negro Problem and Modern Democracy*, almost a generation before, Myrdal pointed out:

> The American Negro problem is a problem in the heart of the American. It is there that the interracial tension has its focus. It is there that the decisive struggle goes on.... The "American Dilemma" is the ever raging conflict between, on the one hand, the valuations preserved on the general plane which we shall call the "American Creed," where the American thinks, talks, and acts under the influence of high national and Christian precepts, and on the other hand, the valuations on specific planes of individual and group living, where personal and local interests; economic, social . . . jealousies; considerations of community prestige and conformity; group prejudice against particular persons or types of people; and all sorts of miscellaneous wants, impulses, and habits dominate his outlook.[6]

How would the nation address and remedy what "scars of centuries" had done to the democratic ideals and aspirations of the nation itself? In his address that June afternoon, President Johnson presumably recognized what the formidable challenge of reform would entail, offering a prescription that would attack the problem at its fundamental core—*that would provide black Americans with the opportunity and the means to participate fully and equitably in the society.*

On August 6, 1965—two months after his commencement address at Howard University and five months after "Bloody Sunday"—Johnson signed into law the most stringent and comprehensive federal voting rights legislation in the nation's history. The president remarked then that the Voting

Rights Act flowed from a "clear and simple wrong." Its long-awaited passage represented the pinnacle of black Americans' prolonged struggle to participate fully and freely in American life and society, as the president so expressed.

The presumption behind the new law was that stringent enforcement of voting rights legislation would remedy the problem of black voters' disfranchisement, especially in the South, where disfranchisement was prevalent and pervasive. And to a great extent, the legislation has met its intended goal, effectively bringing an end to literacy tests and other guileful devices that served as prerequisites to voting.[7]

Yet thirty years after the tumultuous and volatile protest campaigns by blacks and their allies to gain access to the ballot box, the Voting Rights Act—its subsequent amendments, in particular—continues to be the focal point of an immensely complex and contentious political and public policy debate.[8] For one, as a result of congressional hearings held in 1975, the scope of the act was enlarged to protect Hispanics and other language minorities.[9] Furthermore, and perhaps even more consequential, in 1982, the Voting Rights Act was amended again. This time, though, the act's regulatory apparatus was expanded greatly, giving vast authority to staff attorneys and other personnel in the Voting Rights Section of the Department of Justice's Civil Rights Division. The Justice Department has since interpreted the 1982 amendments to mean that wherever possible, *states with sizable black populations should create electoral districts that would give blacks a reasonable chance to elect candidates of their choice—by inference blacks.*[10] And herein lies the mainspring of contention.

Critics charge that today the Voting Rights Act is being implemented in significant and unintended ways that vary considerably from what they regard as the legislation's sole purpose—*to guarantee southern blacks the right to cast ballots.*[11] In this way, "bureaucratic lawyers are reshaping politics from Opelika, Alabama to New York City," law professor Peter Schuck has proclaimed.[12] These amendments, others maintain, really amount to the piecemeal metamorphosis of the Voting Rights Act as an "affirmative action tool in the electoral realm."[13] In other words, *entitlements to representation* pull the nation back from its "cherished ideal of a color-blind society."[14]

On the contrary, say voting and civil rights advocates. The amendments to the 1965 legislation have not fully abated the lack of blacks' equal political opportunity. So while federal voting rights legislation is unequivocal in *not* mandating proportional representation, voting rights proponents assert that the fact that blacks remain significantly underrepresented in elective office (especially at the federal level) is a troubling, if not shameful imperfection in the democratic functioning of this country. And racial discrimination by whites, they argue, still remains a prodigious barrier for black candidates competing in majority-white electoral settings.

Others vehemently disagree with the latter argument in particular, asserting that whites' racial attitudes have liberalized significantly since the 1960s.[15] Abigail Thernstrom, for instance, insists that "whites not only say they will vote for black candidates; they do so."[16] The logic of Thernstrom's argument is as follows: Racism by whites in political contests between black and white candidates is a phenomenon of the past and at best, if occurring in the 1990s, manifests itself in isolated political contests with no generalized or discernible pattern; black candidates are evaluated by the same criteria— individual merit, personal and professional qualifications, political experience, issue stances and personal character—as any white office-seeker. The failure of black office-seekers to be elected in majority-white settings, therefore, is the result of political factors that are nonracial. It follows, then, that the reshaping and redrawing of congressional districts to increase the likelihood of the election of black candidates—a race-conscious remedy mandated by the 1982 amendments to the Voting Rights Act—are both unnecessary and wrong-headed.

What does one make of Thernstrom's claim? Is she right about whites' willingness to cast a ballot for black candidates? That this is a greatly contested issue in the present debate is indeed an understatement. The roster of black officeholders who have won elections with some white support during the last two decades, admittedly, is impressive. For instance, Tom Bradley of Los Angeles, Ernest Morial of New Orleans, Harold Washington of Chicago, David Dinkins of New York, Norman Rice of Seattle, and Ron Kirk of Dallas were the first blacks ever to govern these metropolitan cities.[17] In 1989, Virginian Douglas Wilder became the first black elected governor from a southern state.[18] In 1992, Carol Moseley-Braun of Illinois became the first black woman ever to hold a seat in the United States Senate.[19] And in 1996, Julia Carson was elected to Congress from a white majority district in Indiana.

But does the success of *some* black office-seekers in getting sufficient numbers of whites to vote for them mean that race is no longer an issue? Richard Pildes of the University of Michigan School of Law has written that despite such political gains on the part of black Americans, whites remain less willing because of race to support black candidates for elected office, and any assertion that they are so inclined is "fanciful."[20] Pildes points to the empirical evidence meticulously detailed in *Quiet Revolution in the South: The Impact of the Voting Rights Act, 1965–1990*, which he argues "convincingly demonstrates the increase in black officeholding is not the result of changing attitudes or voluntary reforms."[21] Echoing this sentiment, too, are social scientists Bernard Grofman, Lisa Handley, and Richard Niemi, who point out that the election of blacks to public office from majority-white settings is not that common.[22] The fact is, federal intervention in the form of the Voting Rights Act has been responsible for what participation and representation strides blacks have made in the American electoral process, most notably in the South—despite whites' entrenched hostility to their aspirations for political equality and inclusion historically.

Besides dismantling the legally sanctioned obstacles that whites had long employed to deny blacks their right to register and vote as guaranteed by the Fifteenth Amendment to the Constitution,[23] the Voting Rights Act of 1965 had the immediate and unmistakable effect of increasing the presence of black officials at all levels of elective government. For example, in 1941, the number of black officeholders throughout the United States was a mere 33, as compared to 280 in 1965. As a direct consequence of the sweeping 1965 legislation, black Americans (and southern blacks especially) began registering and, subsequently, electing representatives of their choice. By 1970, in the eleven states of the old Confederacy, the number of black elected officials increased from 776 to an astounding 2,256.[24] Figures compiled by the Joint Center for Political and Economic Studies indicate that more than 8,000 blacks hold public office at the federal, state, city, and county levels, as of this writing.[25]

The nation now seems intent on scurrying toward the ideal of color blindness, particularly in political terms, and thereby proposes to do away with race-conscious remedies within the electoral realm. The presumption is that racial discrimination by whites no longer shapes their political thinking and electoral choices. I, however, believe this is incorrect. Though enormous legal barriers to blacks' electoral participation have fallen, an intractable problem remains: *black political aspirants cannot compete equally or effectively in electoral jurisdictions comprised overwhelmingly of white voters because of the continued vigor of racial prejudice and discrimination.*

It is my contention—and the empirical evidence detailed here will support my view—that the paucity of black officeholders from non-majority-black areas is due in significant part to the continued racial animus underlying whites' political thinking and voting behavior. In the realm of race and political campaigns, aspiring black candidates who must garner the support of white voters are not afforded an equal political opportunity to compete for elected office, especially against the backdrop of racially charged campaign environments. The dispiriting reality is this: black office-seekers who compete in majority-white settings in the main are unable to attract consistent widespread support because *race perniciously influences both the tenor of their electoral campaigns and their outcomes.* Nearly a generation after passage of the most stringent federal voting rights legislation ever, we have yet to adequately and fully address the question of *ensuring equal political opportunity for black political aspirants who compete in majority-white electoral settings.*

This book, then, brings into marked focus probing questions concerning race, equal political opportunity, and the Voting Rights Act:

1. *Given that an overwhelming majority of white Americans endorse the principle of equal opportunity for blacks, how do black office-seekers fare in biracial contests? Do whites afford equal consideration to a black candidate of matched standing as a white candidate?*

2. *How valid is the claim by voting rights advocates that racially polarized voting among whites significantly hinders a black candidate's ability to compete for white votes? Do black candidates who run in majority-white settings lose elections for reasons other than race, or does racial bias remain an intractable obstacle? And if racial considerations on the part of whites exert a role in biracial elections, how does one identify them?*

3. *In its election coverage of biracial campaigns, how does the press cover the story? Does the press inadvertently cue hostile racial sentiments on the part of whites, with unintended though pernicious consequences for black candidates?*

4. *Assuming, by and large, that societal norms now frown on explicit racial appeals in political campaigns, are "subtle" racial appeals in news coverage, for exam-*

ple, effective? If so, how? In what way(s)? What are the likely consequences, if any, concerning a black candidate's electoral viability among white voters?

5. *If whites, in fact, are cued by the press to engage in electoral discriminatory behavior where black candidates are concerned, are blacks not entitled to protection under the Voting Rights Act? Should the scope of the act be enforced to address instances of electoral discrimination faced by black office-seekers if they cannot equally compete in jurisdictions comprised overwhelmingly of white voters?*

These questions, I submit, lie at the center of a larger and no less controversial political and public policy debate: *how permissible is affirmative action in the electoral sphere?*

What follows is not another polemic contribution to the ever growing controversy surrounding the Voting Rights Act. Rather, this study examines the explosive and volatile nature of the distinct nexus between white voters and black candidates—but against the backdrop of racial campaign politics. Hence, *Voting Hopes or Fears?* is a more complex and reasoned story that casts conspicuous doubt on the "color-blind," "color-free" canon many journalists, public officials, academic and political commentators, and those in the electorate at large have so readily pronounced and embraced. It is, in essence, a forthright and provoking story about the enduring nature of racial politics as practiced in America and underscores the continued influence of present-day voting discrimination on black aspirants' equal political opportunity to compete for elected office in this country.

I

OUR
INTRACTABLE
PROBLEM

◆　◆　◆

1

Race—A Political Lightning Rod

♦ ♦ ♦

The voice of the people is but an echo chamber. The output of an echo chamber bears an inevitable and invariable relation to the input. As candidates and parties clamor for attention and vie for popular support, the people's verdict can be no more than a selective reflection from among the alternatives and outlooks presented to them.
—V. O. Key, *The Responsible Electorate*

[T]he levels of support may vary with individual candidates and campaigns. But the evidence is overwhelming that black candidates in the main find it difficult to attract sizable white support.
—Lucius Barker, "Ronald Reagan, Jesse Jackson, and the 1984 Presidential Election"

Election campaign research suggests that the fundamental and distinctive dynamic of a political campaign is its capacity to stimulate, inform, and mobilize potential voters.[1] In the case of any political aspirant seeking elected office, the arduous process of reaching voters is carried out not only by the candidate but also by his or her campaign organization. The organization is able to exert a great deal of influence over the campaign process by devising tactics and strategy; defining the candidate's issue stances; crafting the presentation of his or her personal attributes and image; and, most important, disseminating the necessary information about its candidate. Indeed, much of the information potential voters obtain about candidates and issues during an

13

election contest is furnished by campaign organizations rather than through any direct contact with the individual candidates themselves.[2]

One task of a campaign organization, then, is to define one's opponent and make certain that much of the information over which it has control contains the pertinent "cues." With this task, a candidate's organizational effort provides directional primers or signals such that potential voters might wade through a barrage of campaign information and assess each candidate relative to his or her opponent. It follows, then, that campaign appeals are particularly effective in shaping voters' perceptions of and preferences for those seeking elected office.[3]

Because race has long been such a volatile issue in the United States generally, it has tended to manifest itself in electoral and campaign politics throughout the country.[4] At the same time, political candidates and their staffs have become adept and inventive in the deployment of race-related campaign tactics and strategies to garner white electoral support. In contemporary election campaigns across the country and particularly in the South, when it comes to race, the strategy has been—and continues to be—to campaign about social issues with veiled racial overtones.

That racial prejudice is the easiest and invariably the most effective of all malignancies in American society for political candidates and their campaign operatives to exploit is irrefutable. One need only contemplate the apparent ease with which candidates, on the counsel of strategists and consultants, make explicit and subtle appeals to white voters' racial fears and sentiments. A flagrant though illustrative case in point is the injection of Willie Horton into the 1988 presidential contest between Massachusetts governor and Democratic nominee Michael Dukakis and Republican vice president George Bush. How Horton, a black man and convicted felon, was to figure so prominently in an American presidential election contest is as provocative and controversial as any election strategy in the history of contemporary political campaigns.

In May 1975, William R. Horton Jr. and two companions were sentenced to life in a Massachusetts prison without the possibility of parole for armed robbery and the first-degree murder of a seventeen-year-old gas station attendant.[5] Despite being condemned to a life behind bars, Horton was to benefit from an unusual set of political circumstances—some would later say, bureaucratic foul-ups. For one, his imprisonment coincided with the early stages of a national prisoners' rights movement to which the Democratic Party committed itself in its platform.[6] As early as 1972, Massachusetts governor Francis W. Sargent established the state's inmate-furlough program; a little-known state statute made it possible for first-degree murderers to become eligible for weekend furloughs from prison.

Although he was initially a strong supporter of the furlough program established by his Republican predecessor, in 1976—two years into his first gubernatorial term—Michael Dukakis pocket-vetoed legislation prohibiting furloughs of any kind for first-degree murderers.[7] Though Dukakis was not directly aware of his eligibility, Willie Horton received his tenth weekend furlough in June 1986 and promptly disappeared. He resurfaced on April 3, 1987, at the home of a white couple residing in Oxon Hill, Maryland, where he carried out a vicious attack on the couple, tying the man up and cutting him twenty-two times and brutally raping the man's fiancée.

A year later, Bush's campaign, under the direction of manager and strategist Lee Atwater, aptly used the Horton-furlough fiasco during its presidential face-off with Dukakis. Atwater especially seemed to relish the opportunity to employ "hardball race-coded campaign tactics,"[8] even goading Dukakis two weeks before his party was to convene for its national convention:

> I can't wait until this Dukakis fellow gets down here [the South]. There are quite a few questions he ought to have to answer every day he's down here, and every time he gives the answer, *there's going to be votes coming up just like a cash register.* Can you imagine him trying to answer how in the world as governor, a responsible position like governor, he was in favor of this furlough program that allowed first-degree murderers and drug pushers to go on weekend vacations where they could murder, sell drugs and do all the rest of this stuff? There is a story about a fellow named Willie Horton who for all I know may end up to be Dukakis' running mate . . . maybe he'll put this Willie Horton guy on the ticket after all is said and done. And Willie Horton is the fellow who was a convicted murderer and rapist who got let out on eight [Atwater got the figure wrong] of these weekend furloughs, and on the ninth one, he brutally and wantonly raped this woman. . . . And do you know what the response was from the Dukakis crowd: "Well he didn't do anything on the other eight" [emphasis added].[9]

Having toiled on the 1970 South Carolina senatorial campaign of one-time segregationist Strom Thurmond, Atwater became remarkably adept and inventive in selecting social issues with veiled racial messages. The Horton-furlough campaign tactic was meant to stir and arouse the racial anxieties of white southerners (and white southern Democrats, in particular); the import of Marion Irish's 1942 comments regarding southern politics was not lost on Atwater. "The elementary determinant in Southern politics," Irish wrote, "is an intense Negro phobia which has scarcely abated since Reconstruction."[10]

Grasping the significance of Irish's insight, Atwater went to work, seeking to fracture Dukakis's seventeen-point advantage in midsummer 1988. It was under his direction that the Bush campaign orchestrated a barrage of campaign attacks: speeches, literature, and political advertisements, all featuring Willie Horton and the deficiencies of the Massachusetts furlough program.[11] Kathleen Hall Jamieson, a prominent media scholar and analyst, has commented that such "dirty campaign tactics" served the intended purpose of making Dukakis appear "soft" on crime while simultaneously injecting race into the presidential campaign; she added, "[I]t is not by accident that the image chosen by the Republicans to symbolize the Massachusetts furlough system was a black male."[12]

Though political analysts, scholars, and observers admonished him for the "hardball race-coded campaign tactics" he employed, Atwater's strategy for garnering Republican support in the 1988 presidential campaign seemed to affirm *his belief* in the existence of whites' antiblack sentiments throughout the electorate. Therefore, by invoking the issue of crime with its accompanying veiled racial cues as a prominent campaign theme, the Republicans' intent was as plain as a pikestaff: to arouse the racial prejudices and sentiments of the white electorate against the election of Dukakis as president of the United States.[13] Thomas and Mary Edsall put it this way: "[C]rime [became] a shorthand signal to a crucial group of white voters, for broader issues of social disorder, evoking powerful ideas about authority, status, morality, self-control and race."[14]

While race is often injected into election contests between two white political candidates, in my view, it takes on increased salience in campaigns in which a black and white political aspirant vie for white support. If a white office-seeker can accuse a white opponent of favoring the release of a murderer and rapist (who, as chance would have it, is a menacing black male), while steadfastly maintaining that he is really speaking to the issue of crime, is it not realistic to expect and indeed anticipate that racial appeals—whether overt or subtle—will make their way into an election campaign in which one candidate is white and his or her challenger black?

Consider the following. In the 1990 North Carolina U.S. senatorial contest, Republican incumbent Jesse Helms unveiled a blatantly incendiary ad during the waning days of his hotly contested battle with Democrat Harvey Gantt, a successful black architect and former mayor of Charlotte. Almost a month before voters were to go to the polls, the Helms campaign ran three "race-cueing" television spots, one of which asserted that Gantt had used his mayoral position and minority status to acquire a free television license from the federal government.[15] With Gantt reportedly holding a slight lead over the Republican incumbent Helms in preelection polls conducted some ten days before election day,[16] the senator's campaign organization unleashed perhaps the most racially inciting ad of the entire campaign—the "white hands" spot. Relating the unambiguous racial overture of this Helms advertisement, Professor Jamieson penned this:

> The . . . ad . . . showed the plaid-shirted arms and white hands of a male, a simple gold wedding ring on the third finger of his left hand, opening, presumably reading and then crumbling a rejection letter as the announcer says, "You needed that job, and you were the best qualified. But they had to give it to a minority because of a racial quota. Is that really fair? Harvey Gantt says it is. Gantt supports Ted Kennedy's racial quota law that makes the color of your skin more important than your qualifications. You'll vote on this issue next Tuesday. For racial quotas: Harvey Gantt. Against racial quotas: Jesse Helms."[17]

Helms's employment of the ad, coming so close to election day, sparked a spirited debate in campaign, media, and academic circles. Was the "white hands" commercial merely an ad designed to emphasize that Helms and Gantt might, in fact, hold contrasting policy views on a legitimate campaign issue? Or was it a way to focus attention on Gantt's skin color and, therefore, a pernicious and desperate appeal that pandered to whites' racial hostilities?

Given the dramatic and racially inflammatory theme of the political commercial, did the racial cue in the "white hands" ad resonate with potential white voters? In *Dirty Politics: Deception, Distraction, and Democracy*, Jamieson has suggested that the reaction of white focus group participants was indeed emotional and visceral, as made clear by one such discussant:

"There isn't any Nigra who doesn't think that he's owed a living. Every one of 'em is at the trough with his hand out. We ought to put every one of them in trucks and send them C.O.D. to Jesse Jackson. All I can think of is his [Harvey Gantt's] big black lips and that ugly guy's face. I was willing to think that Harvey Gantt was good, a good black. But after this. No. (pause) No. You just have to resent it when those people who aren't qualified take away our jobs." *Focus group moderator:* "Who do you think is taking jobs?" *[Response]:* "You know, like that guy *[motions to TV screen which is blank]* with Gantt. He's the kind Gantt would give, er, put in charge. Someone who hasn't even gone to school. Can't even, oh, I don't know. They're just taking over, that's all. I know that it sounds prejudiced but I've worked with 'em and they know they can't be fired so their attitude is 'kiss my black ass.' " *Focus group moderator:* "So, you are saying that you've worked with blacks and" *[interrupted]* "Not by choice. I've had trouble. You may as well say I've worked for 'em. That they won't work is a fact, a fact. Go out there and look for yourself. There's a big difference between being prejudiced and being fed up."[18]

With just 52.5 percent of the vote, Helms won reelection to his U.S. Senate seat. Gantt, on the other hand, needed a minimum of 42 percent of the white vote to win but garnered only 38 percent or 981,573 of the 2,677,162 votes cast by white North Carolinians.[19]

One point should be made here, and I make it emphatically. Any inferences drawn from a focus group discussion about whether the "white hands" or any other oppositional spot helped to catapult the senator to victory hold no social scientific reliability. The methodology underlying focus groups does not enable u̅s̅ to demonstrate, let alone conclude with scientific confidence, that whites who harbored antiblack sentiments toward Gantt in fact yielded to those sentiments once they entered the voting booth (this specific issue will be taken up in chapters 2 and 5).

But what the Jamieson focus group discussant's comments do suggest is that one facet of the conversation centered not on Gantt's personal and professional qualifications for elective office or even whether he actually was a proponent of racial quotas. Instead, the onerous suggestion is that Gantt, if elected, might appoint unqualified black people to jobs to which they are not entitled. If the focus group participant's comments yield any valuable insight, it is that the Helms organization evidently achieved some success in *framing the campaign's contextual environment*—consequently, shaping some white North Carolinians' perceptions of Gantt. Harvey Gantt's receptivity—as expressed by the one focus group participant—appears to be conditioned by that individual's antiblack attitudes, opinions, and stereotypes; Gantt is perceived and evaluated accordingly. Of course this leads one to ponder how Gantt, or any other black political aspirant for that matter, can surmount the exploitation of "whispered fears, prejudices privately held but publicly denied."[20]

Recall, too, the sulfurous 1983 Chicago mayoral contest in which black Democratic congressman Harold Washington challenged Bernard Epton, a wealthy Republican. One of many insightful and apt descriptions about the campaign's acerbic racial tenor and its effect on the campaign environment is provided by Paul Kleppner, who writes:

> The attack on his character made Washington the central issue of the campaign. "We've given people a reason to vote against Washington" by concentrating on his past misdeeds [principally, the suspension of his law license in 1970 for not performing work for clients for which he was paid and a 1972 jail term for income tax evasion], one Republican strategist surmised. To convert this anti-Washington sentiment into a vote for the Republican candidate, Epton's television spots ended with what became the most controversial line of the campaign, the slogan "Epton for Mayor— Before It's Too Late!"[21]

In making Washington's character an issue by invoking the "Epton for Mayor" slogan, Epton categorically disavowed that either he or his campaign was appealing to the racial sentiments and fears of white Chicagoans. Kleppner contends, "Epton's negative advertising and sardonic comments didn't create fear and resentment among white ethnic voters. Those sentiments existed long before Epton began his campaign. His strategy tapped those attitudes, served as a rallying point for them."[22]

On reflection, it can be argued also that against the backdrop of deeply entrenched racial divisions in the Chicago electorate, Epton's attack on Washington's character constituted a surreptitious campaign strategy: link Washington's personal disposition and "character failings" to whites' disparaging stereotypes about blacks as a categorical group. To be fair, many whites would affix no racial significance or intent to Epton's oppositional tactics at all. But it is possible— if not probable—that more than a few white Chicagoans were of the opinion that blacks as a categorical group by and large do not possess much personal integrity and character; given that Washington is "one of them," is it not surprising that he would cheat clients or evade paying taxes since this is how "most of them" tend to behave?

By subtly "cueing race," the Epton team was betting heavily that its veiled strategy would arouse the negative characterizations and opinions many white Chicagoans harbored about blacks more generally and would in turn fuel opposition to Washington's candidacy. It nearly succeeded. Despite Epton's coded and in some instances overt appeals to race, Harold Washington became the first black mayor in the history of Chicago—albeit by a scant margin.[23]

One additional point should be raised. I do not mean to leave the impression that every white North Carolinian or Chicagoan or American holds racial antipathy toward blacks, lying in wait for the opportunity to demonstrate it where an aspiring black office-seeker is concerned. Indeed, in their empirical analysis of 1990 survey data, for instance, political psychologists Donald Kinder and Tali Mendelberg demonstrate that whites who harbor the most hostility and disdain toward blacks are southerners, the elderly, and the less well educated.[24] Their empirical conclusions are buttressed, as one will discover, by original data presented and analyzed in later chapters. What I am asserting is that biracial electoral competition, particularly against the backdrop of a racially charged campaign environment, can bring even the most latent antiblack predispositions to the surface. Kleppner, in fact, makes the point quite nicely: "Biracial contests elsewhere may not involve the open and stringent racial appeals that characterized Chicago's mayoral contest. But we should not mistake tone for substance; each biracial contest will bring latent tensions and hostilities to the surface and strain intergroup relations."[25]

Echoing his assessment, too, are political scientists Robert Huckfeldt and Carol Kohfeld, who suggest that

> racial conflict in electoral politics is not simply a consequence of individual attitudes and predispositions. Many Americans are indeed racists and racist attitudes are central to racial conflict, but neither fact *explains* racial conflict. Were there significantly fewer racists in Chicago during the 1979

mayoral election than during the 1983 mayoral election? Probably not, but *conditions* in 1983 provoked levels of racial animosity that were unimagined four years earlier . . . . [R]acial conflict is fundamentally a group phenomenon, subject to environmental and structural properties that are variable through time. Thus, the pattern and consequence of racial conflict in electoral politics must be understood in terms of particular groups at particular times in particular places [emphasis added].[26]

The central point to be made here, then, is this: though political contests between two white candidates may traffic in blatant or subtle appeals to race, *where a black candidate competes against a white opponent in a jurisdiction whose population is comprised overwhelmingly of white voters, race becomes a key factor in the campaign.*

But before moving on to suggest a way of thinking further about the manifestation and salience of race particularly in biracial political campaigns, it is important to define what I mean by the term "racial appeals."

What Is a Racial Campaign Appeal?

According to sociologist Paul Luebke, racial appeals "are present in a campaign if one candidate calls attention to the race of his or her opponent or opponent's supporters or if the news media covering a campaign disproportionately call attention to the race of one candidate or of that candidate's supporters."[27] In addition, I want to suggest that in a biracial campaign, the salience of racial appeals is heightened by the news media through and by "emphasis, nuance, innuendo, and peripheral embellishments,"[28] selected labels, and vocabulary. For instance, reporting that a white challenger's opponent in an election contest is a "black attorney who is seeking to become the district's first black congressman and is a proponent of affirmative action" is one ostensible yet prevalent and routine example of this practice. Such language, media scholar Michael Parenti has written, often "convey[s] positive or negative cues regarding events and persona, often without the benefit of— and usually as a substitute for—supportive information."[29]

As Parenti's comments intimate, campaign appeals that heighten the salience of race are injected into election contests not exclusively by political candidates and their operatives but by news media organizations as well. Political scientists Edie Goldenberg and Michael Traugott have argued that "the dissemination of some information is largely beyond the candidate's control. Reporters and editors produce mass media content in the form of news coverage that is sometimes at odds with campaign intentions."[30]

In light of the increasing role and influence of news media organizations throughout American society, this is an especially crucial point, one aptly recognized by Bernard Cohen decades ago:

> [T]he press is significantly more than a purveyor of information and opinion. *It may not be successful . . . in telling people what to think, but it is stunningly successful in telling its readers what to think about.* And it follows from this that the world looks different to different people, depending not only on their personal interests, but also on the map that is drawn for them by writers, editors, and publishers of the papers they read. Perhaps the notion of a map is too confining, for it does not suggest the full range of the political phenomena that are conveyed by the press. It is, more properly, an atlas of places, personages, situations and events; and to the extent that the press even discusses the ideas that men have for coping with the day's ration of problems, it is an atlas of policy possibilities, alternatives, choices. The editor may believe he is only printing the things that people want to read, but he is thereby *putting a claim on their attention, powerfully determining what they will be thinking about, and talking about, until the next wave laps their shores* [emphasis added].[31]

Given the enormous role of news media in linking voters to politics, news coverage of an office-seeker or officeholder who is black can convey even subtle messages and cues. It follows, then, that overt or subtle racial cues embedded in news coverage purportedly intended to disseminate factual information may trigger negative prejudicial responses among the white electorate.

An insightful illustration of this thesis can be found by examining a lengthy series of investigative stories in the *Detroit Free Press* and the *Detroit News* that became known as the "Magnum and Vista stories." The focus of both news series was an investigation into the conferring of contracts by the city of Detroit. The Magnum news series focused on contracts for the delivery of bus fuel, while the Vista stories concerned the removal of solid waste disposal from a sewage treatment plant. During the period from January 1, 1982, to August 31, 1983, some 686 news stories, columns, and editorials regarding these contract issues appeared between the two papers.[32]

The journalistic merit of this investigative series notwithstanding, the entire affair became "news" alone, primarily as a result of the articles' "exhaustive though racially-biased" tone and content.[33] Specifically, black Detroiters perceived that the papers' white reporters and editors were making racial appeals to white audiences of Detroit's suburban communities and believed that Coleman Young—Detroit's black mayor at the time and his administration were the targets of biased and unfair reporting. In an investigation of the news coverage, media researchers Lee Becker, Thomas Schwartz, and Sharon West concluded:

> The news columns of the two papers contain some clear instances of racist language. Magnum was referred to almost throughout as "minority-owned" or something similar when it seems to have little bearing on the development of the story. . . . Columnist Pete Waldmeir, through his choice of language and style, frequently demonstrates an insensitivity to issues of race. . . . The media seem to have great difficulty recognizing that news by definition is racist. News is what is exceptional. To a white in a dominant society, being black is unusual. Having a black mayor is unusual. . . . In each case, race is the basis for deciding what is unusual, and what is, therefore, news.[34]

While it is not my intention to paint every news media organization with such a broad stroke, Becker, Schwartz, and West indeed are correct in their assessment that race, in many instances, defines what is news; under certain conditions and circumstances, such news content is quite successful in setting public policy and election campaign agendas.

News media organizations, then, in their coverage of electoral competition between black and white political candidates, invariably promulgate the campaign in terms of racial-political conflict as it defines or impedes on campaign strategy and themes.[35] Or journalists and editors, perhaps believing that they are simply reporting interesting aspects of the campaign and the candidates, make continual references to race, most often in the form of adjectives to describe the black office-seeker vis-à-vis his or her white opponent.[36] Hence, given the norms and conventions of news organizations—the rewarding of messages that are dramatic, personal, concise, and visual and that take the form of narrative[37]—race is treated as highly salient in coverage of black candidates' campaigns, thereby making the task of attracting white electoral support, I argue, all the more difficult.

It should now be clear that I part company with the view that if only black political aspirants would campaign aggressively for white electoral support, such support would be forthcoming.[38] Electoral verdicts, political scientist V. O. Key reasoned, are not cast in a vacuum. Quite the opposite. Political decisions rendered by the electorate are more likely the consequence of inputs and stimuli unique to "environmental and structural conditions." Following the logic of Key's argument, I have attempted here to suggest a way of thinking about race as a central and, under particular electoral circumstances, predominant and pernicious factor that still shapes the political thinking and behavior of whites; it plays a volatile role in black candidates' efforts to garner electoral support in majority-white settings.

In short, in addition to a candidate's racial group membership, a constellation of racial factors—antiblack prejudice on the part of the white electorate, the political mobilization of race as a fear appeal, and news campaign coverage that heightens the salience of race—helps to explain the difficulties black political aspirants generally encounter when competing for white votes. Indeed, "race in America serves as a political lightning rod whether the candidates intend it to or not."[39] Therefore, the principal task at hand is identifying whether racial appeals, particularly those embedded in press coverage, influence whites' evaluative judgments and electoral choices in biracial campaigns. This is the subject to which I turn next.

2

Voting Discrimination against Black Candidates

◆ ◆ ◆

Race is a factor. It's there. Every Chicagoan knows it's there.
—Harold Washington, quoted on book jacket of
Paul Kleppner, *Chicago Divided*

On November 2, 1982, Democrat Tom Bradley lost his bid to become the nation's first black elected governor by "the closest proportional margin in the history of California's gubernatorial races, 49.3 percent to 48.1 percent— a mere 93,000 votes out of more than 7.8 million votes cast."[1] Bradley's race-blind, nonthreatening persona notwithstanding, racial appeals permeated the campaign's contextual environment.[2] For one, the campaign organization of Republican George Deukmejian, his opponent, made use of both racist mailings and racially toned political advertisements to garner white electoral support throughout the state, despite a pledge to avoid such racial tactics.[3]

In addition, Bradley's race ostensibly surfaced as an issue in early October, when Bill Rodgers, Deukmejian's experienced campaign manager, remarked to a group of journalists covering the contest, "If we are down only five points or less in the polls by election time, we're going to win. It's just a fact of life. If people are going to vote that way, they certainly are not going to announce it for a survey taker."[4] Political writer John Balzar of the *San Francisco Chronicle* characterized Rodgers's commentary in the following manner:

25

While Rodgers added that the Deukmejian campaign would not raise race as an issue, his comments had the unmistakable effect. And there was a widespread view in political circles that Rodgers, who has handled campaigns for many Republicans, including Ronald Reagan, was too experienced to speak out without knowing what kind of effect his remarks would have.[5]

Social scientists Thomas Pettigrew and Denise Alston observed that a week after Rodgers's rather candid remarks about a probable "latent racial effect" in the Californian electorate, Bradley began losing his comfortable margin over Deukmejian—"dwindling from a safe 12 to the 14 percentage points in early October to an unsafe 3 to 7 percentage points by the end of the month."[6] As table 2.1 shows, exit survey interviews with white Californians suggested that Bradley was "well ahead." But he in fact lost, despite capturing a reported 42 to 43 percent of their votes.[7]

In the previous chapter, I suggested that given the swirl of racial factors in a biracial campaign environment—antiblack prejudicial sentiments on the part of whites; the political mobilization of race as a fear appeal; news campaign coverage that heightens the salience of race—voting discrimination toward a black office-seeker is perhaps inevitable. Of particular interest for this discussion is the fact that no such behavior toward Bradley is observable in the preelection and exit poll data displayed in table 2.1. Consequently, the absence of any discernible anti-prejudicial sentiment led most political analysts and observers to posit that nonracial political factors instead were responsible for Bradley's threadlike gubernatorial loss.[8]

On the other hand, preelection and exit opinion surveys conducted during Harold Washington's Chicago mayoral election—just a year later—offer a vastly striking comparative portrait of whether whites would, in fact, "vote that way." As table 2.2 points out, Washington had the support of no more than 30 percent of whites over the duration of the general election, as compared with Bernard Epton's particularly strong showing. Observe, too, that in the waning days of the campaign, Epton held a 3-to-1 advantage, with nearly 15 percent of whites still undecided. And according to exit poll surveys, white undecided Chicagoans indeed moved to the Epton camp. Despite winning the Chicago mayoralty, Washington did so with just 12.3 percent of white support.[9] "More than any other factor," Paul Kleppner concluded, "race dominated voting choices."[10]

TABLE 2.1. Preference Polls of White Registered Voters: California 1982 Gubernatorial Race (August 1981 to November 1982)

Date and Polling Organization			Percentage of Respondents		
Field Institute	Tarrance & Associates	Teichner Associates	For Bradley	For Deukmejian	Undecided or Others
August 1981	—	—	55%	31%	14%
October 1981	—	—	54	33	13
January 1982	—	—	50	39	11
—	January 1982	—	53	32	15
March 1982	—	—	50	40	10
May 1982	—	—	52	39	9
Early June 1982	—	—	49	44	7
June 8, 1982ᵃ	—	—	45	42	13
August 1982	—	—	47	38	15
October 1–4, 1982	—	—	53	39	8
—	October 7, 1982	—	49	37	14
—	—	October 9–10, 1982	50	37	13
—	October 14, 1982	—	45	41	14
—	October 21, 1982	—	45	41	14
October 24–26, 1982	—	—	47	41	12
October 29–31, 1982	—	—	49	42	13
—	November 1, 1982	—	45	42	9
November 2, 1982ᵇ	—	—	"Bradley	Well	Ahead"
Election day results	—	—	48.1	49.3	2.6

Source: Adapted from Thomas E. Pettigrew and Denise A. Alston, *Tom Bradley's Campaign for Governor: The Dilemma of Race and Political Strategies* (Washington: Joint Center for Economic and Political Studies, 1988), p. 12.

ᵃ indicates primary election exit interviews.
ᵇ indicates election exit interviews.

TABLE 2.2. Preference Polls of White Registered Voters: Chicago 1983 Mayoral Race (March to April 1983)

Interview Dates	Washington	Epton	Undecided
March 15[a]	25%	39%	37%
March 22[b]	18	41	41[e]
March 24[b]	27	55	17
March 26–30[c]	20	64	16
March 29[a]	18	58	25
April 5[b]	20	61	18
April 10[a]	20	66	14
April 12[d]	19	81	—
April 12[b]	23	77	—

Source: Adapted from Paul Kleppner, *Chicago Divided: The Making of a Black Mayor* (DeKalb: Northern Illinois University Press, 1985), p. 204.

Note: Entries are percentages and each row sums to 100 percent, except for rounding error.

[a]Preelection poll conducted by Richard Day Research, Inc.
[b]Preelection poll conducted by Market Shares, Inc. and the April 12 results are from the WBBM-TV (CBS) exit poll.
[c]Preelection poll conducted by the Gallup Organization.
[d]WMAQ-TV (NBC) exit poll.

I submit, however, that among whites who are prejudiced against blacks, we do not know with certainty whether racial considerations play a role in their aversion to cast a ballot for a black office-seeker. In California's 1982 gubernatorial contest, for instance, no negative prejudicial sentiments were manifested in the preelection and exit survey data, while data from the 1983 Chicago mayoralty only suggest that race *may* have been an explanatory factor in the electoral outcome. Indeed, these two case studies aptly illustrate the fundamental conundrum in attempting to corroborate the contested claim that whites' voting behavior in biracial political contests is often motivated by racial animus.

To put the matter more forthrightly, the majority of whites in the electorate know that societal norms now frown on blatant displays of discriminatory behavior, such as opposing a black office-seeker simply on the basis of skin color. Robert Axelrod, for instance, has presented a compelling argument about the evolution and stability of established norms.[11] He argues that because norms govern our political and social lives, individuals are for the most part bound to abide by them or risk being sanctioned in some way. It follows from this that openly exhibiting racially discriminatory behavior might cause white voters to be branded "racists" or "bigots" in light of the current political and social climate.

Even so, a sizable minority appears not to be at all apprehensive about expressing an unwillingness to vote for a black candidate simply because he is black. Certain researchers, for example, reported that although an overwhelming majority of whites indicate that they would have no problem voting for a qualified black candidate running for president of the United States, fully 25 percent of whites indicated that they would *not* vote for such a candidate.[12]

For whites, voting in any political contest is a concealed, perhaps even camouflaged activity, especially when the choice of candidates includes a black office-seeker. A voter can enter the voting booth, make a candidate selection, exit, and find herself greeted by a pollster inquiring about her vote choice. She can either accurately report for whom she voted or provide an account that varies from her actual behavior. The simple fact of the matter is that given the privacy of the ballot, political analysts are relegated to drawing inferences about individual voting behavior from aggregate voting statistics—particularly cross-registration and turnout figures. Using data of this sort to assess whether whites' evaluative judgments and political choices are affected by, say, racial appeals, one is beset with specific limitations; the most serious one is that these data do not provide us with direct information about what motivates one's candidate selection.[13] Thus, it is difficult to discern the reason(s) for whites' political choices in a biracial contest. I am suggesting—and I want to be clear on this point—that *in the absence of direct information about the motivations and sentiments underlying individual voting behavior, the claim that whites disregard race on entering the voting booth remains more of an assertion than a rigorously established empirical fact.* Carol Swain has appropriately characterized the problem this way:

> According to conventional wisdom, black candidates lose in such areas [majority-white settings] because of the racism of white voters. At present, knowledge about why voters sometimes vote along racial lines . . . is defi-

cient. What we know is based on a handful of comparative studies of local governmental elections and case studies of statewide races of Tom Bradley, Douglas Wilder and Edward Brooke.[14]

I am not contending, however, that black office-seekers on every occasion always lose elections for reasons of race. Though "we can assume that race is always a factor"[15] in biracial political campaigns—whether it is overtly discernible or not—to date, it has been fairly difficult to establish what influence, if any, the racial animus in a biracial campaign environment exerts on whites' receptivity toward a black political aspirant. Indeed, given the secrecy of the vote, some have argued that proving discriminatory intent by whites is nearly impossible.[16]

The remainder of this chapter describes a research design strategy that helps unmask the privacy of the ballot while at the same time moving us beyond a mere case study appraisal. The goal is to discern whether racial considerations on the part of whites influence their evaluative judgments and political choices where black office-seekers are concerned.

The Case for Methodological Pluralism

Recall that my inquiry here is limited to the issue *of assessing the significance of racial appeals*—particularly those embedded in print news coverage—for both the tenor of black candidates' political campaigns and their electoral outcomes. I address the following questions: In its campaign coverage, is there a discernible pattern of the print media's calling attention to the race of one candidate or of that candidate's supporters? If so, how prevalent is the practice? What racial "cues," if any, are conveyed? Is the tone of print news campaign coverage positive, neutral, or negative? To what degree do whites harbor anti-prejudicial sentiments toward blacks as a categorical group? Against the backdrop of whites' hostile racial sentiments, do racial appeals embedded in print news campaign coverage have unintended though pernicious consequences for a black office-seeker attempting to garner white electoral support?

To *empirically* assess interrelated questions of this sort requires the deployment of a research study design that encompasses both qualitative and quantitative strategies. And I employ two specific social science techniques here: content analysis of print news campaign coverage and, most important, a social experiment[17] that involves the incorporation of experimental manipulations of print news campaign stories within a public opinion survey of voting-age adults.[18]

What Can Content Analysis of Print News Campaign Coverage Tell Us?

Because content analysis enables a researcher to conduct a systematic assessment of the *content* of communication, an empirical investigation of the patterns of newspaper campaign coverage of biracial elections can indeed shed light on questions concerning the presence, frequency, and tone of racial appeals. The inquiry here specifically uses content analysis data to both ascertain and contrast the presence of racial appeals in print news coverage of two biracial election campaigns in 1989 from vastly different electoral settings: the New York mayoral contest in which black Democratic candidate and former Manhattan borough president David Dinkins opposed Republican nominee and U.S. District Attorney Rudolph Giuliani, and the Seattle mayoralty race between veteran city councilman Norman Rice, also a black Democrat, and his Republican challenger, city attorney Doug Jewett.

The content analysis data analyzed and collected by trained coders encompass news articles, editorials, opinion columns, and letters to the editor. In the case of the 1989 Dinkins–Giuliani match-up, the data come from the *New York Times's*[19] coverage of the race, while data pertaining to the 1989 Rice-Jewett mayoral contest were drawn from news coverage provided by the *Seattle Times*. For a fuller description of the design and coding procedures regarding these content analysis data, consult appendix A.

What Can a Social Experiment Embedded in a Public Opinion Survey Tell Us?

In *Whose Votes Count?: Affirmative Action and Minority Voting Rights Policy,* Abigail Thernstrom has noted, "Black candidates, like white ones, lose elections for a variety of reasons, including insufficient support from black constituents, the power of incumbency, inadequate name recognition, age, experience, reputation, and political orientation."[20] Of course, one might also add to such a listing other campaign factors: campaign strategy and tactics, financial contributions or lack thereof to one's organizational effort, news media and other campaign endorsements, type of office being sought, and voters' racial and political predispositions, in addition to other ascriptive attributes of the candidates themselves—for instance, gender or personal character. As I have suggested, aggregate voting returns or preelection and exit polling data in biracial elections more often than not provide evidence *suggesting* the existence of an interrelationship between a myriad of campaign factors and the degree of white electoral support a black political aspirant garners.

Still, as physical and social scientists are inclined to point out, "correlation is not causation." That a black candidate garners a mere 12 percent of the white vote in a biracial mayoral contest against the backdrop of evidence documenting the pervasiveness of racial appeals in the campaign unfortunately does not answer the question, What was the impact of those appeals? Identifying and demonstrating the actual and precise influence of this particular causal relationship is a fundamentally different, though not entirely unfeasible task. Indeed, discerning the causal link between racial campaign appeals and whites' evaluative judgments and political choices requires that a showing be made that racial appeals, independent of other factors, are responsible for whites' aversion to supporting that black candidate. As difficult as it may seem given the complexity of a multitude of electoral campaign factors that exert an influence on individual voting behavior, suspected causal relationships can be shown by the deployment of *carefully controlled experimental methods.*

The principal strength of the carefully controlled experiment to test for "what causes what" is that it affords an investigator a powerful advantage: by employing procedures of randomization, and treatment and control conditions, one is able to proffer reliable inferences about causality. Donald Kinder and Thomas Palfrey explain:

> By creating treatment and control conditions, the experimenter is able to isolate one causal variable at a time. This, in turn, allows complex phenomena to be decomposed in a way that is impossible under more passive research strategies. Experimenters need not wait for natural processes to provide crucial tests and telling comparisons: they can create them on their own. In this respect, experimental control confers a whopping comparative advantage.[21]

What can we learn about *the public* from experimental studies of, at most, 100 individuals? A lot, we think.[22]

Therefore, to find out whether racial campaign appeals embedded in print news campaign coverage actually shape whites' receptivity toward black political aspirants, I deployed a social experiment that involved the incorporation of experimental manipulations of campaign news stories within a public opinion survey of voting-age adults. Because this approach is a bit unusual, I wish to describe the nature of the experiment and the manipulations in greater detail here.

First, a representative cross section of white individuals residing in the state of Michigan was interviewed as part of a face-to-face public opinion survey.[23] This initial study specifically sought to examine the links among racial attitudes, racial residential segregation, and labor market inequalities. The questions regarding labor market inequalities aside, respondents also were asked approximately forty attitudinal questions—all pertaining to race. In addition, individuals were queried about their identification with political parties and ideological predispositions. Standard demographic information such as education, income, gender, and religious orientation was collected as well. Given the primary foci of the study, only household members twenty-one years of age and older were considered as eligible respondents. Because these personal interviews were based on a *carefully selected probability sample of voting-age adults*, no aspect in either the selection of housing units or actual respondents was left to the discretion of an interviewer.[24]

Approximately six months later, each of the white respondents interviewed in the face-to-face opinion survey was randomly assigned to receive a brief mail questionnaire containing *one* of four contrived news campaign stories.[25] Respondents were informed (in the stem introducing the news article) that the story appeared in a newspaper from another state.[26] Each campaign story depicted an especially negative-spirited, *nonpartisan* mayoral election contest between two fictitious candidates: Arthur Christopher, a well-respected businessman and former head of the city's chamber of commerce, and Gregory Hammond, a fifteen-year veteran of the city council.

The text of the news article that appears in figure 2.1 makes a reference to the fact that Christopher and Hammond hold contrasting policy stances regarding environmental policy; candidate Hammond is depicted as a pru-

Headline. **Candidates Disagree on The Environment**
Byline. Thomas Young
    Staff Press Writer

The nonpartisan mayoral race entered its final hours with the candidates, local businessman Arthur Christopher and longtime city councilman Gregory Hammond answering voters' questions during a well-attended town meeting last night.

What began as a clash of visions and personalities, by evening's end, had taken on a more amiable tone as members of the audience pleaded with them to focus on issues and dispense with the negative attacks that have marked the campaign thus far.

Though a wide array of questions from education to government services was posed to the candidates, a question regarding the environment elicited the sharpest disagreement between Christopher and Hammond during the evening.

David Carnes, an unemployed laborer, asked the candidates to explain their position on stringent fuel-efficiency standards. Christopher, 47, who is white, said that he opposes implementing higher standards. "My opponent's radical environmental policies would cost jobs, plain and simple." Hammond, 45, *who is also white*, retorted that Christopher continues to misrepresent his position. "I believe it is possible to have a strong environmental policy that should not threaten jobs," Hammond said.

Both Christopher and Hammond noted that they are well-suited to tackle the city's growing deficit. Christopher cited his longtime business experience and five-year involvement with the city's chamber of commerce, which has helped bring jobs to the area. Hammond, on the other hand, said that his 15 years on the council make him the most qualified to address the city's increasingly complex problems.

FIGURE 2.1   Text of News Campaign Stimuli in Experimental Study. *Note*: The change in wording is italicized. Copyright © 1994 by Keith Reeves. All rights reserved.

Headline. **Candidates Disagree on The Environment**
Byline. Thomas Young
Staff Press Writer

The nonpartisan mayoral race entered its final hours with the candidates, local businessman Arthur Christopher and longtime city councilman Gregory Hammond answering voters' questions during a well-attended town meeting last night.

What began as a clash of visions and personalities, by evening's end, had taken on a more amiable tone as members of the audience pleaded with them to focus on issues and dispense with the negative attacks that have marked the campaign thus far.

Though a wide array of questions from education to government services was posed to the candidates, a question regarding the environment elicited the sharpest disagreement between Christopher and Hammond during the evening.

David Carnes, an unemployed laborer, asked the candidates to explain their position on stringent fuel-efficiency standards. Christopher, 47, who is white, said that he opposes implementing higher standards. "My opponent's radical environmental policies would cost jobs, plain and simple." Hammond, 45, *who is seeking to become the city's first black mayor,* retorted that Christopher continues to misrepresent his position. "I believe it is possible to have a strong environmental policy that should not threaten jobs," Hammond said.

Both Christopher and Hammond noted that they are well-suited to tackle the city's growing deficit. Christopher cited his longtime business experience and five-year involvement with the city's chamber of commerce, which has helped bring jobs to the area. Hammond, on the other hand, said that his 15 years on the council make him the most qualified to address the city's increasingly complex problems.

FIGURE 2.2   Text of News Campaign Stimuli in Experimental Study. *Note:* The change in wording is italicized. Copyright © 1994 by Keith Reeves. All rights reserved.

dent *proponent of fuel efficiency standards.* Observe, however, that the text of the news article that appears in figure 2.2 is nearly identical, save for one important detail: candidate Hammond's race was changed. This particular campaign story reported that he is "seeking to become the city's first black mayor." Thus, in the two news campaign articles that described the mayoral candidates' stances on environmental policy, one story depicted a same-race contest in which both mayoral candidates are white, while the other news story described a biracial contest, in which one office-seeker is white and his opponent black.

By contrast, the news information that appears in the campaign stories displayed in figures 2.3 and 2.4 is nearly identical, though the primary focus is both candidates' issue stances on affirmative action—a more racially charged campaign theme. Again, the print news campaign coverage depicted both a same-race and a biracial mayoral contest. Note, though, that Hammond is depicted as a *conditional proponent of affirmative action.* "I favor affirmative action programs as a remedy when there has been an identifiable history of discrimination by an employer," Hammond was reported to have said. And here, too, the news story about the biracial contest mentioned that he is "seeking to become the city's first black mayor."

Finally, each print news campaign article concluded by mentioning limited biographical information such as the candidates' age, professional qualifications, and experience. Thus, the four news campaign stories given to the white participants differed only along two dimensions: *the mention of the candidates' race and the mention of a prominent campaign theme—affirmative action or the environment.* As one can readily see, all other central campaign information was not varied.

Again, the underlying rationale of these experimental manipulations was to assess the influence of 'subtle' racial campaign appeals embedded in print news campaign coverage under systematically varied electoral circumstances. For a more detailed account of the recruitment and randomization procedures, also consult appendix B.

Demographic and Political Profile of Experiment Participants

Table 2.3 indicates that the 253 participants in the experimental study indeed comprised a cross section of the general population: the age of the individ-

Headline. **Candidates Disagree on Affirmative Action**
Byline. Thomas Young
    Staff Press Writer

    The nonpartisan mayoral race entered its final hours with the candidates, local businessman Arthur Christopher and longtime city councilman Gregory Hammond answering voters' questions during a well-attended town meeting last night.

    What began as a clash of visions and personalities, by evening's end, had taken on a more amiable tone as members of the audience pleaded with the candidates to focus on issues and dispense with the negative attacks that have marked the campaign thus far.

    Though a wide array of questions from education to the environment was posed to the candidates, a question regarding affirmative action elicited the sharpest disagreement between Christopher and Hammond during the evening.

    David Carnes, an unemployed laborer, asked the candidates to explain their position on affirmative action. Christopher, 47, who is white, said that he opposes affirmative action programs. "Quotas are not the answer. My opponent's support of affirmative action programs amounts to quotas, plain and simple." Hammond, 45, *who is also white*, retorted that Christopher continues to misrepresent his position. "I favor affirmative action programs as a remedy when there has been an identifiable history of discrimination by an employer," Hammond said.

    Both Christopher and Hammond noted that they are well-suited to tackle the city's growing deficit. Christopher cited his longtime business experience and five-year involvement with the city's chamber of commerce, which has helped bring jobs to the area. Hammond, on the other hand, said that his 15 years on the council make him the most qualified to address the city's increasingly complex problems.

FIGURE 2.3 Text of News Campaign Stimuli in Experimental Study. *Note:* The change in wording is italicized. Copyright © 1994 by Keith Reeves. All rights reserved.

Headline. **Candidates Disagree on Affirmative Action**
Byline. Thomas Young
   Staff Press Writer

The nonpartisan mayoral race entered its final hours with the candidates, local businessman Arthur Christopher and longtime city councilman Gregory Hammond, answering voters' questions during a well-attended town meeting last night.

What began as a clash of visions and personalities, by evening's end, had taken on a more amiable tone as members of the audience pleaded with the candidates to focus on issues and dispense with the negative attacks that have marked the campaign thus far.

Though a wide array of questions from education to the environment was posed to the candidates, a question regarding affirmative action elicited the sharpest disagreement between Christopher and Hammond during the evening.

David Carnes, an unemployed laborer, asked the candidates to explain their position on affirmative action. Christopher, 47, who is white, said that he opposes affirmative action programs. "Quotas are not the answer. My opponent's support of affirmative action programs amounts to quotas, plain and simple." Hammond, 45, *who is seeking to become the city's first black mayor*, retorted that Christopher continues to misrepresent his position. "I favor affirmative action programs as a remedy when there has been an identifiable history of discrimination by an employer," Hammond said.

Both Christopher and Hammond noted that they are well-suited to tackle the city's growing deficit. Christopher cited his longtime business experience and five-year involvement with the city's chamber of commerce, which has helped bring jobs to the area. Hammond, on the other hand, said that his 15 years on the council make him the most qualified to address the city's increasingly complex problems.

FIGURE **2.4**   Text of News Campaign Stimuli in Experimental Study. *Note*: The change in wording is italicized. Copyright © 1994 by Keith Reeves. All rights reserved.

TABLE 2.3. Demographic and Political Profile of Experiment Participants

Age		Gender	
21–29 years	13%	Male	40%
30–39	29	Female	60
40–49	18		
50–64	16		
65–92	23		
Average:	48 years		
Education		Place of residence	
High school or less	46%	Suburbs	85%
Some college	28	Detroit city	15
College graduate	13		
Post-college	12		
Party identification		Ideology	
Democrat	27%	Extreme liberal	2%
Independent	27	Liberal	23
Republican	27	Moderate	38
Other/no preference	18	Conservative	30
		Extreme conservative	2
Television viewing		Newspaper reading	
None	2%	None	10%
One–three days	13	One–three days	26
Four–six days	30	Four–six days	22
Every day	52	Every day	39
Average	6 days	Average	5 days

Source: 1992 Biracial Election Campaign Study.

Note: Percentages in some cases do not equal 100 due to missing data.
Number of participants=253.

uals ranged from 21 to 92 years; 40 percent of the subjects were men, while 60 percent were women. Eighty-five percent resided in suburban communities, and more than half had attended college. An array of political and ideological orientations is reflected in the sample as well. Democrats, Republicans, and Independents were equally represented in the study group, with 27 percent in each party identification category. Eighteen percent reported other or no partisan preference. Twenty-five percent of the respondents classified themselves as liberal, and 38 percent claimed to be moderates, while 32 percent self-identified as conservatives. In addition, respondents as a group were avid consumers of news information: the average number of days viewing television news in the previous week was six, compared to an average of five days reading the newspaper.

Racial Attitudinal Profile of Experiment Participants

In addition, table 2.4 shows the distribution of responses made by the experiment participants when queried directly about their explanations concerning persisting black-white socioeconomic inequalities. Taken together, these data tend to support the claim that a considerable segment of whites in our study harbors antiblack sentiments. [27] For instance, while 55 percent strongly or somewhat agreed with the statement "Black people have worse jobs, education, and housing than white people because of racial discrimination," 42 percent somewhat or strongly disagreed. Moreover, when presented with a question regarding whether blacks lack educational opportunities, a slightly higher percentage of respondents disagreed (50 percent) either somewhat or strongly. Half the sample, too, concurred with the assertion that blacks lack the motivation and the Protestant work ethic to pull themselves out of poverty. And when asked about whether they believe blacks as a group have an inclination to collect welfare rather than work, nearly five out of ten

TABLE 2.4. Racial Attitudinal Profile of Experiment Participants

[1] *Black people have worse jobs, education, and housing than white people because of racial discrimination.*

	N	Percentage
Strongly Agree	34	13%
Somewhat Agree	104	41
Somewhat Disagree	66	26
Strongly Disagree	41	16

[2] *Black people have worse jobs, education, and housing than white people because most blacks have less inborn ability to learn.*

	N	Percentage
Strongly Agree	11	4%
Somewhat Agree	44	17
Somewhat Disagree	44	17
Strongly Disagree	150	60

TABLE 2.4. *(continued)*

[3] *Black people have worse jobs, education, and housing than white people because most blacks don't have the chance for education it takes to rise out of poverty.*

	N	Percentage
Strongly Agree	41	16%
Somewhat Agree	83	33
Somewhat Disagree	73	29
Strongly Disagree	52	21

[4] *Black people have worse jobs, education, and housing than white people because most blacks don't have the motivation or willpower to pull themselves out of poverty.*

	N	Percentage
Strongly Agree	43	17%
Somewhat Agree	95	38
Somewhat Disagree	58	23
Strongly Disagree	49	20

[5] *In general, how much discrimination is there that hurts the chances of blacks to get jobs?*

	N	Percentage
A lot	84	33%
Some	100	40
Only a little	36	14
None at all	25	10

[6] *Now I have some questions about different groups in our society. I'm going to show you a seven-point scale on which the characteristics of people in a group can be rated. . . . Where would you rate blacks on this scale, where 1 means "tends to prefer to be self-supporting" and 7 means "tends to live off welfare"?*

	N	Percentage
1 (*Self-supporting*)	18	7%
2	20	8
3	21	8
4	58	23
5	68	27
6	34	13
7 (*Prefers welfare*)	16	6

Source: 1992 Biracial Election Campaign Study.

Note: The percentages do not equal 100 in some cases due to missing data.
Number of participants=253.

whites agreed. At the same time, an overwhelming majority of whites rejected the notion that blacks are innately inferior (77 percent disagreed that blacks have less inborn ability to learn) and acknowledged that blacks do encounter some or a lot of racial discrimination.

In summary, employing a multifaceted methodological strategy such as the one undertaken in the present study enables a researcher to "escape the limitations inherent in any single approach."[28] These limitations, of course, are well-known to physical and social scientists engaged in empirical investigation. Although this methodological strategy does not solve all potential limitations, it does allow for the investigation of interrelated questions from a number of equally rich vantage points. The methodological portfolio employed in the present study—in particular, the use of experimental manipulations of print campaign news information within a public opinion survey—should lead to a richer description of political and social reality[29] and enable us to draw broader conclusions about both the existence of racial campaign appeals on the part of print media and the political effectiveness of such appeals. I now turn to the empirical evidence.

II

THE
EMPIRICAL
EVIDENCE

◆ ◆ ◆

3

The Print Press—
Making an Issue of Race

◆ ◆ ◆

I did not have to make any references to race because the newspaper said, "Mickey Michaux, black attorney from Durham, North Carolina, seeking to become the first black congressman,"—I mean every newspaper article, every TV story. The media made an issue of race.
— Henry "Mickey" Michaux, quoted in Thomas E. Cavanagh, ed.,
Race and Political Strategy

That is the problem. By just letting them label you, you leave the white candidate an open field to shape race as a variable.
— Thomas Pettigrew, quoted in Thomas E. Cavanagh, ed.,
Race and Political Strategy

The injection of race into an election contest in which a black and white candidate oppose each other serves as strategic technique that is meant to mobilize whites to discriminate against a black office-seeker, I have argued. What is more, the media tend to be handmaidens to such campaign strategies and tactics. Most black office-seekers recognize that political competition against a white opponent generally ensures great interest and attention on the part of the news media. News coverage of their electoral bids is superficial at best, and polarizing at worst, for journalistic norms and conventions prescribe that stories, events, and persona that are either potentially influential or emanate controversy and conflict are newsworthy.[1] And by referring

45

to Mickey Michaux, David Dinkins, Norman Rice, Carol Moseley-Braun, or Tom Bradley as "a black candidate," the media inadvertently send cues that shape white voters' subjective evaluations. Whether inadvertent or not, the cueing of race by the press shapes both the tenor of biracial political campaigns and their outcomes.

Consider, if you will, the self-reported candidate preferences of whites in the 1989 New York mayoral election, shown in figure 3.1. As the data indicate, according to the earliest preelection poll (August 26–29, 1989), David Dinkins had the support of 37 percent of white voters; Rudolph Giuliani's share was 32 percent. On the other hand, almost 18 percent of whites indicated a preference for a candidate other than Dinkins or Giuliani; those who answered "don't know" constituted 13 percent of the vote share.

What is most striking about these data is that as the mayoral election

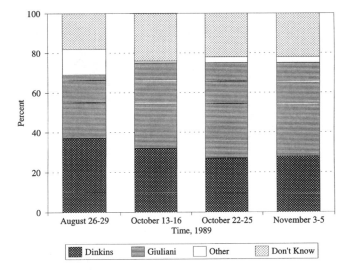

FIGURE 3.1   Preference Polls of White Registered Voters: New York 1989 Mayoral Race (August to November 1989). *Note:* The data reported here are weighted. Gallup conducted two preelection polls for 1 (August 26–29, N=1,012; October 22–25, N=1,411). Gallup also conducted two polls for Fox (October 13–16, N=1,261; November 3–5, N=4,305).

campaign progressed, Dinkins's support among whites eroded significantly—from 37 percent in August to just 28 percent, according to a preelection survey conducted just two days before election day. Conversely, Giuliani's vote share among white New Yorkers actually increased about 15 percentage points. Observe, too, that at the time the last preelection poll was conducted (November 3–5), the percentage of undecided whites was a substantial 20 percent. Were racial campaign appeals in news campaign coverage responsible in part for the steady decline of support for Dinkins among likely white voters?

Recall that an election contest is characterized by racial campaign appeals if one candidate calls attention to the race of his or her opponent or opponent's supporters or if the press covering the campaign disproportionately call attention to the race of one candidate or of that candidate's supporters.[2] Consider, then, excerpts from news coverage of the 1989 New York and Seattle mayoralty elections by the *New York Times* and the *Seattle Times*, respectively:

> After nearly 100 whites have presided over the City Hall, including two Jewish mayors in succession for the last 16 years, Mr. [David] Dinkins would be the first black.[3]

> Race, up to now an undertone in the Seattle mayoral campaign, is showing signs of rising to the surface. . . . [Doug] Jewett, who is white, faces black City Councilman Norm Rice in the general election in November. The SOS [Save Our Schools] initiative [to end mandatory school busing in Seattle], which Jewett helped draft, is also on the November ballot.[4]

Other campaign stories, for instance, read as follows:

> New Yorkers need no reminder that he [Dinkins] would be the city's first black mayor and while he won 3 in 10 voters among whites in the Democratic primary, the pool of whites is larger in the general election. . . . Mr. [Rudolph] Giuliani's hopes seemed to be tied to the letter C: crime, crack, corruption, compassion, competence, character, color, [Robert] Carson [a controversial Dinkins campaign aide who is black and a convicted felon], cronyism, credibility.[5]

> It illustrates the problem of being a black politician in a city with an overwhelmingly white voting majority—voters Rice needs if he is to win next

week. Certainly the core of his strength is in the legislative districts with the highest minority populations—the 37th and 43rd in central and South Seattle. But it is essential he do well in such predominantly white districts as the 36th and 32nd in North Seattle.[6]

These selected excerpts of print news coverage are illustrative in that they might be taken as evidence of racial campaign appeals on the part of the press. To be fair, such excerpts actually provide limited insight—if any— about whether either paper engaged in the practice of routinely making an issue of race in its election coverage. Indeed, the excerpts offer neither a systematic nor a representative *empirical* assessment about the frequency, pattern, and tone of racial campaign appeals by the print press. For example, was there a discernible and consistent pattern by either the *New York Times* or the *Seattle Times* of calling attention to race? If so, how prevalent was the practice? What racial cues were conveyed? Was the overall tone of these cues positive, neutral, or negative?

To answer such questions, this chapter presents evidence from our content analysis of print news coverage of the New York and Seattle mayoralty elections in 1989.

Presented in figure 3.2 is the total distribution of all campaign-related news items about the mayoral race between David Dinkins and Rudolph Giuliani collected and analyzed from the *New York Times*. The figure shows that 13 percent of the 326 items comprised opinion columns, editorials, and letters to the editor, while 87 percent of the campaign coverage consisted of news stories. By contrast, the data in figure 3.3 indicate that the coverage by the *Seattle Times* of that city's mayoral race was of a vastly different pattern: of the 211 campaign-related items, 42 percent consisted of editorials, opinion columns, and letters to the editor, as compared with only 58 percent of news articles. That the overall pattern in each paper's election coverage was skewed in the direction of news suggests that both print news organizations actually ascribed relative importance to news analysis of each mayoral contest.

Next, shown in figures 3.4 and 3.5 is the percentage of news *stories* that appeared over the course of each paper's coverage. In figure 3.4 for instance, the overall pattern reveals that as election day neared, press attention to the New York mayoral race increased. In the waning weeks of the Dinkins-

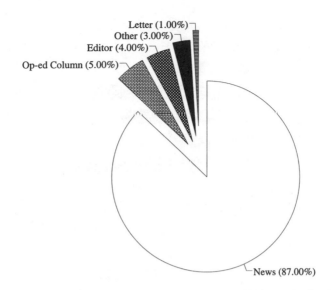

FIGURE 3.2   Type of Print news Campaign Coverage, 1989 New York Mayoral Election. *Source:* Content Analysis Study.

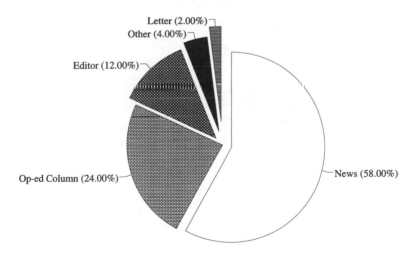

FIGURE 3.3   Type of Print News Campaign Coverage, 1989 Seattle Mayoral Election. *Source:* Content Analysis Study.

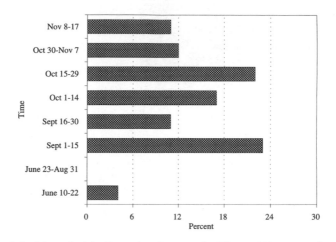

FIGURE 3.4 News Article Campaign Coverage by Time, 1989 New York Mayoral Election. *Source:* Content Analysis Study.

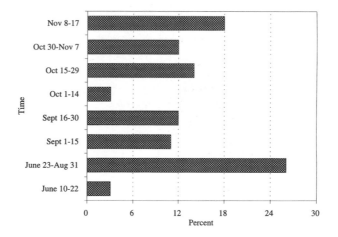

FIGURE 3.5 News Article Campaign Coverage by Time, 1989 Seattle Mayoral Election. *Source:* Content Analysis Study.

Giuliani race, coverage by the *New York Times* practically snowballed; 62 percent of all mayoral race stories appeared between September 16 and November 7 (election day). In comparison, 51 percent of all campaign stories about Seattle mayoral candidates Norman Rice and Doug Jewett appeared in the *Seattle Times* during this same time period. Observe, too, that postelection analysis by the *New York Times* of the mayoral race in New York tapered off, while the *Seattle Times*'s coverage of that city's mayoral contest did not.

In sum, our content analysis data illustrate two rather interesting descriptive findings about press coverage of two 1989 biracial mayoral campaigns—which occurred in two staunchly Democratic, yet vastly different cities. First, much of the election coverage consisted primarily of analysis in the form of campaign news stories, as compared with, say, editorials or letters to the editor. Second, and also not surprising, the sheer quantity of this coverage, as measured by the *frequency* of news stories, was related to the progression of each mayoral campaign. As election day approached, each paper's attention to that city's mayoral race increased accordingly.

Considering the increased media interest and attention that black-white political competition typically engenders, one might expect that each newspaper's campaign coverage would emphasize race principally. Yet according to figures 3.6 and 3.7, there is only partial support for this particular hypothesis. While the primary emphasis of 2 percent of the 256 news stories from the *New York Times* was poll-related (i.e., projections about "who's ahead, who's behind"), 20 percent did focus on race entirely; a mere 2 percent principally addressed both preelection polls and race. By contrast, data from the *Seattle Times* suggest that 9 percent of its 123 news stories focused entirely on race. Thus, the overwhelming majority of news campaign stories from both papers (73 percent and 89 percent, for the *New York Times* and the *Seattle Times*, respectively) *did not* focus on race per se.

Although figures 3.6 and 3.7 point out that neither the *New York Times* nor the *Seattle Times* emphasized race primarily in its election news coverage, I want to suggest that a more intricate racial "cueing" dimension can be examined—language. Media scholar Michael Parenti reminds us about its importance: "One common framing method is to select labels and other vocabulary designed to convey politically loaded images. These labels and phrases . . . convey positive or negative cues regarding events and persona, often without the benefit of—and usually as a substitute for—supportive

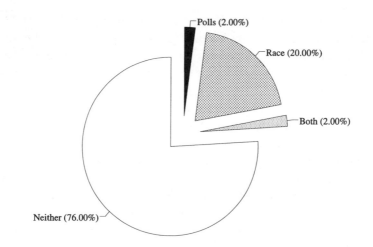

FIGURE 3.6 Primary Focus of News Article Campaign Coverage, 1989 New York Mayoral Election. *Source:* Content Analysis Study.

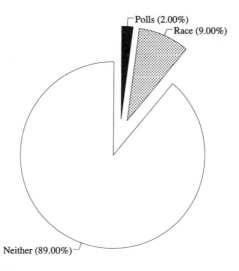

FIGURE 3.7 Primary Focus of News Article Campaign Coverage, 1989 Seattle Mayoral Election. *Source:* Content Analysis Study.

information."[7] This hypothesis, if applied to print news coverage of biracial elections, suggests that the language in campaign coverage may contain both overt and subtle "primers and signals" about race.

First, the data displayed in figure 3.8 make clear that in 20 percent of news stories by the *New York Times*, the language included a specific reference to either Dinkins's race or Giuliani's Italian heritage—presumably "peripheral embellishments" that contributed very little substantive information. In marked contrast, 63 percent of the *Seattle Times*'s coverage, as shown in figure 3.9, referred specifically to the race of one or both of that city's mayoral candidates.

Additionally, figure 3.10 shows that nearly three-quarters of all campaign-related stories in the *New York Times* contained an explicit reference to specific racial or ethnic groups in the New York electorate—blacks, whites, Hispanics, Italians, and Jews. On the other hand, slightly more than a third of all news stories from the *Seattle Times* mentioned racial or ethnic groups that comprised that city's electorate (see figure 3.11).

Further still, the "racial language" hypothesis can be assessed in a second manner—by the number of specific racial references appearing in each *paragraph*. The examination of news coverage patterns along this dimension clearly indicates that employment of racial language by the *New York Times* was prominent and substantial. For instance, as figure 3.12 highlights, 17 percent of all paragraphs contained at least one reference to either the race or ethnicity of a mayoral candidate, politician, or celebrity; a racial or ethnic group in the electorate; or race as it pertained to election campaign strategy. Fourteen percent of all news stories included at least two paragraph references to race. Meanwhile, 6 percent of all paragraphs contained at least three racial references, while 7 percent mentioned race at least four times. The typical *New York Times* paragraph, on average, contained seven racial references. An especially notable paragraph was this one:

> In the Post interview, Mr. [Roger] Ailes [the media consultant to the Giuliani campaign] was also asked whether there was a parallel between Mr. [Robert] Carson [a Dinkins campaign consultant and convicted felon] and Willie Horton, the convict used in a television commercial for President Bush's 1988 campaign. "They're both felons, and they're both blacks, but that's not my fault," Mr. Ailes said.[8]

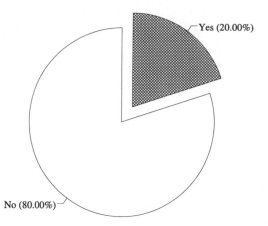

FIGURE 3.8   References to Candidate's Race and Ethnicity in News Article Campaign Coverage, 1989 New York Mayoral Election. *Source:* Content Analysis Study.

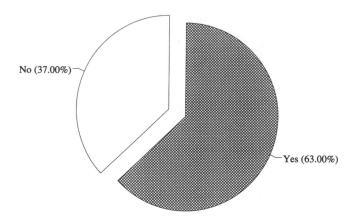

FIGURE 3.9   References to Candidates' Race and Ethnicity in News Article Campaign Coverage, 1989 Seattle Mayoral Election. *Source:* Content Analysis Study.

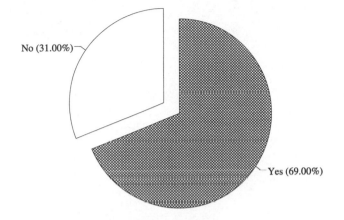

FIGURE 3.10   References to Racial and Ethnic Groups in News Article Campaign Coverage, 1989 New York Mayoral Election. *Source:* Content Analysis Study.

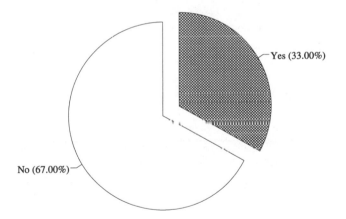

FIGURE 3.11   References to Racial and Ethnic Groups in News Article Campaign Coverage, 1989 Seattle Mayoral Election. *Source:* Content Analysis Study.

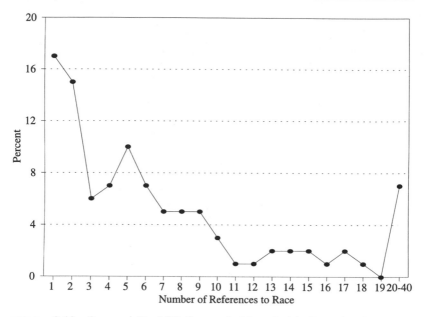

FIGURE 3.12 Paragraph Racial References in News Article Campaign Coverage, 1989 New York Mayoral Election. *Source:* Content Analysis Study.

In contrast, as figure 3.13 shows, 19 percent of all paragraphs in news stories by the *Seattle Times* contained at least one reference to the race or ethnicity of the mayoral candidates; the race of governmental leaders, officials, or celebrities; racial or ethnic groups in the electorate; and race as it pertained to a campaign issue or strategy. One such paragraph included the following racial reference: "During his congressional race last year, Rice started keeping a journal, chronicling his experiences in public life. If he wins Tuesday, he can pen what it's like to the Seattle's first black mayor. If he loses, he can write a postscript about his years on the City Council, because he says he won't run for the council again when his term ends in 1991."[9] Meanwhile, 17 percent of all paragraphs in the *Seattle Times* included at least two racial references, as compared with 12 percent that mentioned race at least three times.

Finally, and perhaps most important, the overall tone of the racial references uncovered here was assessed. This is worthy of examination particularly because the tone of racial appeals in news coverage, I have argued, can make

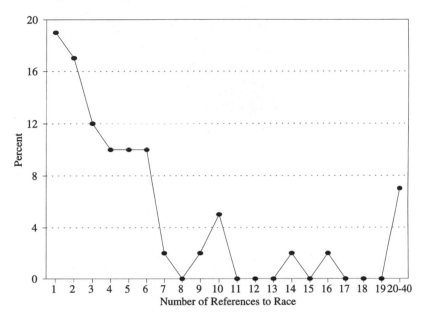

FIGURE 3.13 Paragraph Racial References in News Article Campaign Coverage, 1989 Seattle Mayoral Election. *Source:* Content Analysis Study.

the task of attracting white electoral support all the more difficult for black office-seekers.

If the data displayed in figures 3.14 and 3.15 are any indication, it appears that on the whole, both newspapers did adhere to standard journalistic norms and conventions concerning objectivity, fairness, and balance. Of the 174 campaign news stories from the *New York Times* (see figure 3.14) whose tone was evaluated, 76 percent were neutral, and nearly 6 percent were potentially positive. And given the racial divisiveness that marred the 1989 Dinkins-Giuliani mayoral campaign in particular, one cannot gloss over the fact that nearly 17 percent of all stories in the *New York Times* were potentially or clearly negative with regard to tone.

By contrast, the tone of racial references in news stories by the *Seattle Times* suggests a different pattern (see figure 3.15). Our trained coders determined that in 54 percent of the articles, the tone was neutral. They also concluded that the tone of racial references in 20 percent of the campaign stories

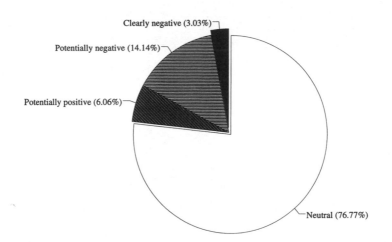

FIGURE 3.14 Tone of Racial References in News Article Campaign Coverage, 1989 New York Mayoral Election. *Source:* Content Analysis Study.

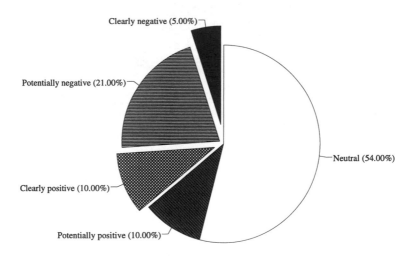

FIGURE 3.15 Tone of Racial References in News Article Campaign Coverage, 1989 Seattle Mayoral Election. *Source:* Content Analysis Study.

was either potentially or clearly positive. However, in slightly more than a quarter (26 percent) of the news articles, the tone of the racial references was potentially or clearly negative.

Rather than take selected excerpts of print news coverage as prima facie evidence of subtle racial campaign appeals, I have used content analysis to proffer a more systematic assessment regarding the presence, frequency, and tone of such appeals. The principal findings—which point in slightly different directions—can be summarized as follows:

- While the overwhelming majority of news stories in both the *New York Times* and the *Seattle Times* did not focus on race primarily, both newspapers did engage in the practice of calling attention to the race of mayoral candidates and their campaign supporters. Twenty percent of stories in the *New York Times* contained a specific reference to either David Dinkins's race or Rudolph Giuliani's Italian heritage. More than 60 percent of stories from the *Seattle Times* specifically made mention of the race of that city's mayoral candidates—Norman Rice and Doug Jewett.
- Three-quarters of campaign stories in the *New York Times* contained a specific reference to racial or ethnic groups in the New York electorate. Slightly more than a third of such references were found in the *Seattle Times*.
- Many of the *paragraphs* in both newspapers contained specific references to race. In the *New York Times*, 17 percent of all paragraphs included at least one racial reference, as compared with 19 percent in the *Seattle Times*.
- Regarding the tone of such references to race, 17 percent of all campaign-related news *stories* from the *New York Times* were potentially or clearly negative, as compared to 26 percent in the *Seattle Times*.

That the press has the uncanny ability to shape race as a variable and thereby undercut one's appeal as a candidate was not lost on Mickey Michaux during his 1982 campaign for a U.S. congressional seat.[10] Nor did this point escape an exasperated Tom Bradley, who during his second bid for the governorship of California lamented, "People tend to think of me as the black mayor of Los Angeles, not as the mayor of Los Angeles who happens to be black. . . . *I am not the black candidate for governor. I am the Democratic party's candidate for governor* [emphasis added].[11]

Given the primordial capacity of the news media to mold and condition public thinking—especially in the volatile arena of race and politics—one critical question follows: can the effectiveness of racial appeals embedded in news campaign coverage be shown given the privacy of the ballot? Such a question of course raises the issue of causal inference, which content analysis data are incapable of establishing. Because of this particular limitation, I now turn to the evidence from our social experiment to determine whether subtle appeals to race by the press can actually provoke whites' fears about black officeholding.

4

The Persistence
of Racial Prejudice
in the Electorate

◆ ◆ ◆

[N]egative characterizations of blacks remain prevalent in contemporary American society notwithstanding the changes that have taken place, and . . . contrary to the conventional wisdom, these negative racial characterizations are openly and routinely expressed.

—Paul Sniderman and Thomas Piazza, *The Star of Race*

It must now be obvious that of particular concern for our analysis is the widespread persistence of racial prejudice in the electorate. Put most simply, despite the positive changes that have occurred with regard to whites' racial attitudes in particular,[1] are black Americans still "the subject of fear, hatred, and distaste"?[2] And must it be admitted that the root and branch of racial prejudice throughout American society are inexorable? Indeed, when one lends an ear to some of our study participants' explanations for why blacks and whites reside in different residential areas, for instance, the answer is a resounding yes.

> Why do I think that [blacks and whites live in different areas] happens? I think blacks, a lot of them, don't keep up their homes. They tend to hang out on street corners instead of in school where they belong. More drugs, alcohol problems. Whites don't want to be around them.[3]

Because they [blacks] are different. The two races have different ideas as to their responsibilities to a neighbor. [Tell me more.] A "black neighborhood" versus a "white neighborhood" is dirtier, less maintained, more inclined to be abused by the residents—throw garbage out the back door and kicking windows out.[4]

Because I think that the majority aren't enthused, not motivated and don't care. I don't know what I want to say. The opportunity is there if they want to take advantage. I don't think most blacks want to work for anything.[5]

Importantly, these direct quotes—which are proffered as illustrative and not representative—range from positing that blacks in the main are bad neighbors to more general characterizations about blacks' personal behavior.[6] In short, this kind of qualitative evidence reminds us of the continued inclination of whites to rely on negative attitudes, opinions, and stereotypes about black Americans as a categorical group. And where political candidates and their campaign staffs or news organizations overtly or subtly stir such prejudices, is it likely that a black office-seeker competing in an overwhelmingly white jurisdiction will be above suspicion as "one of them"? Quite frankly, the very kind of hardened sentiments voiced by these study participants is what gives race-baiting campaign tactics their enormous and pernicious political power.

So it is necessary to ask, To what degree do whites harbor antiblack animosities? This chapter—in a more rigorous empirical fashion—explores that very question.

To recap: before our study-participants were given contrived news campaign stories to read, and in the face-to-face opinion survey they were asked an array of questions about the persisting socioeconomic gulf between blacks and whites. These data, you may recall, were first presented in chapter 2. There we found that whites, by and large, continue to harbor implacable hostility toward blacks. Indeed, the striking variation in responses to the racial attitudinal items shown in table 2.4 leads us to ask whether certain respondent-level attributes influence the degree to which whites harbor such antiblack sentiments; if so, which ones are predominant?

Table 4.1, for instance, describes the cross-tabular relationship between whites' explanations of racial disparities and educational attainment. Note

TABLE 4.1. The Relationship between Whites' Racial Attitudes and Education

1 *Black people have worse jobs, education, and housing than white people because of racial discrimination.*

	Strongly Agree	Somewhat Agree	Somewhat Disagree	Strongly Disagree
High school or less	8%	40%	28%	24%
Some college	11	44	31	14
College graduate	20	42	25	13
Post-college	30	48	18	4

2 *Black people have worse jobs, education, and housing than white people because most blacks have less inborn ability to learn.*

	Strongly Agree	Somewhat Agree	Somewhat Disagree	Strongly Disagree
High school or less	6%	28%	19%	47%
Some college	5	11	18	66
College graduate	—	3	16	81
Post-college	—	15	19	66

3 *Black people have worse jobs, education, and housing than white people because most blacks don't have the chance for education it takes to rise out of poverty.*

	Strongly Agree	Somewhat Agree	Somewhat Disagree	Strongly Disagree
High school or less	13%	27%	32%	27%
Some college	11	35	31	23
College graduate	23	39	26	12
Post-college	30	48	19	3

4 *Black people have worse jobs, education, and housing than white people because most blacks don't have the motivation or willpower to pull themselves out of poverty.*

	Strongly Agree	Somewhat Agree	Somewhat Disagree	Strongly Disagree
High school or less	8%	23%	48%	21%
Some college	18	26	34	21
College graduate	39	19	36	6
Post-college	33	26	33	7

5 *In general, how much discrimination is there that hurts the chances of black people to get good paying jobs?*

	A Lot	Some	A Little	None at All
High school or less	26%	41%	16%	16%
Some college	33	46	14	6
College graduate	42	36	16	6
Post-college	56	33	11	—

TABLE 4.1. (*continued*)

⁶ *Now I have some questions about different groups in our society. I'm going to show you a seven-point scale on which the characteristics of people in a group can be rated. . . . Where would you rate blacks on this scale, where 1 means "tends to prefer to be self-supporting" and 7 means "tends to live off welfare"?*

	1	2	3	4	5	6	7
	Self-Supporting						*Welfare*
High school or less	7%	6%	5%	21%	34%	21%	6%
Some college	6	8	10	33	24	10	9
College graduate	10	12	19	19	29	7	3
Post-college	11	19	15	26	22	3	3

Source: 1992 Biracial Election Campaign Study.

Number of participants=253.

Note: The percentages do not equal 100 in some cases due to missing data.

that on five of the six attitudinal measures, white respondents with more formal education significantly differ from their less well educated counterparts in their beliefs about why blacks lag behind them economically. As compared with less well educated whites, college graduates were more than twice as likely to have strongly endorsed the statement "Blacks have worse jobs, education, and housing than white people because of racial discrimination." Similarly, when queried about how much discrimination hurts the chances of blacks to get jobs that pay well, college-educated whites were almost twice as likely to report "a lot" as compared with individuals with a twelfth-grade education or less (only 26 percent indicated "a lot"). And while 39 percent of college-educated respondents concurred with the statement that blacks have a tendency to rely on welfare assistance rather than be self-supporting, 61 percent of those with a high school diploma or less education agreed. Meanwhile eight out of ten college graduates strongly rejected the idea that blacks are innately inferior, while among their less well educated counterparts, only about five out of ten did so. On the other hand, 58 percent of the study participants who earned a college degree strongly or somewhat agreed that most blacks lack the motivation to succeed, as compared with just 31 percent of those with a high school diploma or less schooling. With one exception, then, whites with more formal education were more empathetic toward blacks' socioeconomic plight and their inability to get ahead.

TABLE 4.2. The Relationship between Whites' Racial Attitudes and Age

[1] *Black people have worse jobs, education, and housing than white people because of racial discrimination.*

	Strongly Agree	Somewhat Agree	Somewhat Disagree	Strongly Disagree
21–29 years	20%	53%	20%	7%
30–39	12	42	29	17
40–49	13	36	38	13
50–64	16	51	14	19
65–92	10	36	28	26

[2] *Black people have worse jobs, education, and housing than white people because most blacks have less inborn ability to learn.*

	Strongly Agree	Somewhat Agree	Somewhat Disagree	Strongly Disagree
21–29 years	10%	7%	20%	63%
30–39	2	9	17	72
40–49	5	8	15	72
50–64	3	16	24	57
65–92	4	46	18	32

[3] *Black people have worse jobs, education, and housing than white people because most blacks don't have the chance for education it takes to rise out of poverty.*

	Strongly Agree	Somewhat Agree	Somewhat Disagree	Strongly Disagree
21–29 years	10%	43%	30%	17%
30–39	15	37	25	23
40–49	13	28	35	23
50–64	30	32	24	14
65–92	14	30	35	21

[4] *Black people have worse jobs, education, and housing than white people because most blacks don't have the motivation or willpower to pull themselves out of poverty.*

	Strongly Agree	Somewhat Agree	Somewhat Disagree	Strongly Disagree
21–29 years	30%	23%	37%	10%
30–39	20	30	34	16
40–49	18	35	40	7
50–64	14	18	49	19
65–92	13	13	45	29

[5] *In general, how much discrimination is there that hurts the chances of black people to get good paying jobs?*

	A Lot	Some	A Little	None at All
21–29 years	33%	47%	20%	—
30–39	32	44	18	6

TABLE 4.2. (*continued*)

40−49	35	45	10	10
50−64	41	38	16	5
65−92	30	36	10	24

[6] *Now I have some questions about different groups in our society. I'm going to show you a seven-point scale on which the characteristics of people in a group can be rated. . . . Where would you rate blacks on this scale, where 1 means "tends to prefer to be self-supporting" and 7 means "tends to live off welfare"?*

	1	2	3	4	5	6	7
	Self-Supporting						Welfare
21−29 years	10%	10%	17%	17%	26%	10%	10%
30−39	8	14	9	27	32	7	3
40−49	12	7	3	35	35	3	5
50−64	8	—	11	27	24	19	11
65−92	2	8	10	16	27	29	7

Source: 1992 Biracial Election Campaign Study.

Number of participants=253.

Note: The percentages do not equal 100 in some cases due to missing data.

Regarding the relationship between whites' explanations of socioeconomic inequality and age, table 4.2 shows that older and younger whites significantly differed on four of the six survey items. Older whites were more likely than younger whites to express the belief that blacks are inherently less intelligent: only 17 percent of 21- to 29-year-old whites endorsed such an assessment, while half of the respondents over the age of 65 did. Older respondents were also less willing to agree that discrimination affects blacks' ability to better themselves economically. And regarding whether blacks have a propensity to prefer welfare, 63 percent of whites age 65 and older tended to agree, as compared with 46 percent of whites age 21 to 29 and 42 percent of whites age 30 to 39.

The relationship between whites' predispositions toward blacks and gender is much less dramatic, as table 4.3 highlights. There is no significant difference in the explanations of racial disparities proffered by white men and women on four of the six attitudinal items. The two items on which men and women's beliefs differed discernibly, however, are whether blacks are innately inferior intellectually and the amount of discrimination that impedes blacks' ability to land a good job at good wages.

TABLE 4.3. The Relationship between Whites' Racial Attitudes and Gender

[1] *Black people have worse jobs, education, and housing than white people because of racial discrimination.*

	Strongly Agree	Somewhat Agree	Somewhat Disagree	Strongly Disagree
Male	16%	40%	28%	16%
Female	11	44	27	18

[2] *Black people have worse jobs, education, and housing than white people because most blacks have less inborn ability to learn.*

	Strongly Agree	Somewhat Agree	Somewhat Disagree	Strongly Disagree
Male	6%	11%	23%	60%
Female	3	23	15	59

[3] *Black people have worse jobs, education, and housing than white people because most blacks don't have the chance for education it takes to rise out of poverty.*

	Strongly Agree	Somewhat Agree	Somewhat Disagree	Strongly Disagree
Male	14%	32%	32%	22%
Female	17	35	27	20

[4] *Black people have worse jobs, education, and housing than white people because most blacks don't have the motivation or willpower to pull themselves out of poverty.*

	Strongly Agree	Somewhat Agree	Somewhat Disagree	Strongly Disagree
Male	24%	17%	40%	19%
Female	14	28	40	17

[5] *In general, how much discrimination is there that hurts the chances of black people to get good paying jobs?*

	A Lot	Some	A Little	None At All
Male	28%	49%	17%	6%
Female	37	36	14	13

[6] *Now I have some questions about different groups in our society. I'm going to show you a seven-point scale on which the characteristics of people in a group can be rated. . . . Where would you rate blacks on this scale, where 1 means "tends to prefer to be self-supporting" and 7 means "tends to live off welfare"?*

	1 Self-Supporting	2	3	4	5	6	7 Welfare
Male	10%	7%	10%	24%	27%	13%	9%
Female	6	10	9	26	30	14	5

Source: 1992 Biracial Election Campaign Study.

Number of participants=253.

Note: The percentages do not equal 100 in some cases due to missing data.

Finally, tables 4.4 and 4.5 describe the cross-tabular relationships between whites' explanations of racial socioeconomic differences and party affiliation and ideological orientation, respectively. In table 4.4 only one question item displayed a statistically significant difference—and just marginally so: "How much discrimination is there that hurts the chances of black people to get good paying jobs?" Forty percent of white Democrats indicated "a lot," as compared with 33 percent of Independents, 34 percent of Republicans, and 24 percent who classified themselves as having no preference for either of the two major political parties.

As table 4.5 reveals, liberals, moderates, and conservatives differed significantly on only one survey item as well—namely, whether blacks have the motivation and willpower to pull themselves up out of poverty. These data indicate clearly that white liberals were comparatively more likely to perceive blacks rather sympathetically. Indeed, 32 percent of self-identified liberals strongly disagreed with the statement that blacks do not possess the motivation to better their station in life, as compared with just 10 percent of moderates and 16 percent of conservatives.

I wish to raise an important caveat regarding our discussion thus far. Researchers have documented that when white Americans are asked to offer an explanation for blacks' lagging socioeconomic fortunes, they consistently endorsed themes suggesting that blacks, and not the federal government or whites, are culpable for their own problems and difficulties.[7] This explanation—known as "attributional blame" in social science parlance—posits that the problems faced by blacks are the result of their own doing, or lack thereof.[8] Whites who sanction this view, for example, tend to believe that racial inequality exists because blacks either are innately inferior intellectually or lack the motivation and willpower to pull themselves out of poverty. Underlying attributional blame explanations for racial inequality, then, is the idea that the purported shortcomings of blacks are due to "deficiencies in character and capabilities."[9] The following questions asked of our study participants fall under this rubric:

- Black people have worse jobs, education, and housing than white people because most blacks have less inborn ability to learn;
- Black people have worse jobs, education, and housing than white people because most blacks don't have the motivation or willpower to pull themselves out of poverty;

TABLE 4.4. The Relationship between Whites' Racial Attitudes and Party Affiliation

[1] *Black people have worse jobs, education, and housing than white people because of racial discrimination.*

	Strongly Agree	Somewhat Agree	Somewhat Disagree	Strongly Disagree
Democrat	15%	48%	18%	19%
Independent	15	34	34	17
Republican	13	45	24	18
No preference	12	41	32	15

[2] *Black people have worse jobs, education, and housing than white people because most blacks have less inborn ability to learn.*

	Strongly Agree	Somewhat Agree	Somewhat Disagree	Strongly Disagree
Democrat	7%	16%	21%	56%
Independent	2	24	20	54
Republican	2	19	18	61
No preference	6	14	11	69

[3] *Black people have worse jobs, education, and housing than white people because most blacks don't have the chance for education it takes to rise out of poverty.*

	Strongly Agree	Somewhat Agree	Somewhat Disagree	Strongly Disagree
Democrat	19%	32%	21%	27%
Independent	14	34	34	18
Republican	16	35	35	14
No preference	17	37	17	26

[4] *Black people have worse jobs, education, and housing than white people because most blacks don't have the motivation or willpower to pull themselves out of poverty.*

	Strongly Agree	Somewhat Agree	Somewhat Disagree	Strongly Disagree
Democrat	15%	40%	26%	19%
Independent	18	44	21	18
Republican	24	32	26	18
No preference	11	49	23	17

[5] *In general, how much discrimination is there that hurts the chances of black people to get good paying jobs?*

	A Lot	Some	A Little	None at All
Democrat	40%	37%	8%	15%
Independent	33	49	9	9
Republican	34	31	23	11
No preference	24	56	14	6

TABLE **4.4.** (*continued*)

[6] *Now I have some questions about different groups in our society. I'm going to show you a seven-point scale on which the characteristics of people in a group can be rated. . . . Where would you rate blacks on this scale, where 1 means "tends to prefer to be self-supporting" and 7 means "tends to live off welfare"?*

	1 Self-Supporting	2	3	4	5	6	7 Welfare
Democrat	10%	10%	7%	29%	24%	17%	3%
Independent	10	5	3	32	29	14	7
Republican	2	9	14	20	31	14	10
No preference	9	14	17	14	31	9	6

Source: 1992 Biracial Election Campaign Study.

Number of participants=253.

Note: The percentages do not equal 100 in some cases due to missing data.

- I'm going to show you a seven-point scale on which the characteristics of people in a group can be rated. . . . Where would you rate blacks on this scale, where 1 means "tends to prefer to be self-supporting" and 7 means "tends to live off welfare"?

In contrast, a second explanation proffered for the widening socioeconomic gap between blacks and whites is "situational blame," again in social science parlance. Here the line of reasoning invokes the notion that the plight of blacks is largely the consequence of the contextual circumstances in which they find themselves. That is, blacks are less likely to realize their socioeconomic aspirations because of the lack of access to quality education, decent housing, employment opportunities, and so forth. Interestingly, the situational blame perspective—unlike attributional blame—tends to acknowledge racial discrimination as a fundamental determinant of blacks' inability to get ahead. So our survey items that fall under the situational blame rubric[10] are as follows:

- Black people have worse jobs, education, and housing than white people because of racial discrimination;
- Black people have worse jobs, education, and housing than white people because most blacks don't have the chance for education it takes to rise out of poverty;
- In general, how much discrimination is there that hurts the chances of black people to get good paying jobs?

TABLE 4.5. The Relationship between Whites' Racial Attitudes and Ideological Orientation

[1] *Black people have worse jobs, education, and housing than white people because of racial discrimination.*

	Strongly Agree	Somewhat Agree	Somewhat Disagree	Strongly Disagree
Liberal	20%	43%	29%	8%
Moderate	12	46	25	17
Conservative	11	37	32	20

[2] *Black people have worse jobs, education, and housing than white people because most blacks have less inborn ability to learn.*

	Strongly Agree	Somewhat Agree	Somewhat Disagree	Strongly Disagree
Liberal	2%	18%	14%	66%
Moderate	3	20	19	57
Conservative	6	15	22	57

[3] *Black people have worse jobs, education, and housing than white people because most blacks don't have the chance for education it takes to rise out of poverty.*

	Strongly Agree	Somewhat Agree	Somewhat Disagree	Strongly Disagree
Liberal	21%	42%	21%	16%
Moderate	12	34	36	18
Conservative	16	27	30	26

[4] *Black people have worse jobs, education, and housing than white people because most blacks don't have the motivation or willpower to pull themselves out of poverty.*

	Strongly Agree	Somewhat Agree	Somewhat Disagree	Strongly Disagree
Liberal	30%	11%	27%	32%
Moderate	22	44	24	10
Conservative	19	44	21	16

[5] *In general, how much discrimination is there that hurts the chances of black people to get good paying jobs?*

	A Lot	Some	A Little	None at All
Liberal	40%	46%	10%	4%
Moderate	31	41	15	13
Conservative	32	39	17	12

TABLE 4.5. (*continued*)

⁶ *Now I have some questions about different groups in our society. I'm going to show you a seven-point scale on which the characteristics of people in a group can be rated. . . . Where would you rate blacks on this scale, where 1 means "tends to prefer to be self-supporting" and 7 means "tends to live off welfare"?*

	1 Self-Supporting	2	3	4	5	6	7 Welfare
Liberal	14%	11%	14%	28%	18%	8%	7%
Moderate	5	8	6	27	34	15	5
Conservative	7	8	11	20	32	13	9v

Source: 1992 Biracial Election Campaign Study.

Number of participants=253.

Note: The percentages do not equal 100 in some cases due to missing data.

For our purposes here, I am interested in whether both attributional and situational blame explanations—in the presence of subtle racial campaign appeals—influence the way whites regard a black office-seeker who competes in a biracial contest. To this end, the effects of respondent-level attributes on the various attributional and situational explanations proffered for racial inequality are shown in tables 4.6 and 4.7, respectively. Table 4.6 indicates a negative association between education and whites' endorsement of the attributional blame explanations. Specifically, college-educated whites, as compared with those with less formal schooling, were less likely to concur that blacks (1) have less of an inborn ability to learn; (2) lack the motivation or willpower to pull themselves out of poverty; (3) are more inclined to depend on welfare than to work. Older study participants, however, were more likely to have endorsed all of the attributional blame explanations for racial inequality. Meanwhile, whites who self-identified as conservatives (as compared with self-identified liberals) concurred only with the notion that blacks tend to live off welfare rather than work. Although gender was negatively related to each attributional explanation, neither relationship was statistically significant.

As the results in table 4.7 point out, education, too, exerted a statistically significant effect on the likelihood of whites' endorsing a situational blame explanation for persisting racial inequality. For instance, those who are col-

TABLE 4.6. The Effect of Respondent-Level Attributes on Attributional Explanations for Racial Inequality

Independent Variable	Blacks Have Less Inborn Ability to Learn	Blacks Lack Motivation	Blacks Prefer Welfare
Education	–.19***	–.30***	–.32***
	(.06)	(.06)	(.10)
Age	.14***	.08*	.20***
	(.04)	(.05)	(.08)
Gender (Women)	–.09	–.06	–.18
	(.12)	(.13)	(.22)
Ideology	.05	.06	.15*
	(.05)	(.05)	(.08)
Constant	1.46***	2.64***	3.81***
	(.28)	(.30)	(.52)
Adjusted R²	.12	.13	.10

Source: Analysis of 1992 Biracial Campaign Election Study.
  Minimum N=232.

Note: Table entries are ordinary least squares coefficients. The standard errors are noted in parentheses. The racial attitudinal variables are coded such that a positive score indicates that one is more likely to *endorse* that particular sentiment. For example, the more formal education one has, the less likely one is to endorse the notion that "blacks have less of an inborn ability to learn."
*p ≤.10, one-tailed test.
***p ≤.01, one-tailed test.

lege-educated were more likely to agree that (1) racial discrimination in fact hurts blacks' chances to get jobs that pay well; (2) blacks have worse jobs, education, and housing than whites because of such discrimination; (3) blacks are not afforded the educational opportunities that would help lift them out of poverty. On the other hand, white men were more likely than white women to reject the latter argument, particularly. Finally, the more conservative one is, the more likely one is to reject both the notion that racial discrimination hurts blacks' chances to get good jobs and the notion that blacks fare worse than whites because of such discrimination.

To reiterate, then, the majority of our study participants indeed ascribed negative attitudes, opinions, and characterizations to black Americans; educational attainment, age, political ideology, and, in one particular instance, gen-

TABLE 4.7. The Effect of Respondent-Level Attributes on Situational Explanations for Racial Inequality

Independent Variable	Blacks Have Worse Jobs . . . Because of Discrimination	Blacks Don't Have the Chance for Education to Rise out of Poverty	Discrimination Hurts Chances to Get Jobs
Education	-.26★★★	-.30★★★	-.23★★★
	(.06)	(.06)	(.06)
Age	.04	-.01	.05
	(.04)	(.05)	(.04)
Gender (Women)	-.06	-.24★	-.03
	(.12)	(.13)	(.12)
Ideology	.08★	.07	.09★
	(.05)	(.05)	(.05)
Constant	2.52★★★	2.98★★★	1.94★★★
	(.28)	(.30)	(.29)
Adjusted R²	.09	.10	.08

Source: Analysis of 1992 Biracial Campaign Election Study.
   Minimum N=232.

Note: Table entries are ordinary least squares coefficients. The standard errors are noted in parentheses. The racial attitudinal variables are coded such that a positive score indicates that one is more likely to *reject* that particular sentiment. For instance, the more conservative one is, the more likely one is to reject the argument that "black people have worse jobs, education, and housing than white people because of racial discrimination."
★p ≤.10, one-tailed test.
★★★p ≤.01, one-tailed test.

der significantly influence the degree to which whites harbor antiblack sentiments.

   Before concluding, I should like to emphasize again a point I made in earlier chapters. I do not mean to imply that all whites hold negative attitudes and characterizations about blacks.[11] Indeed, our findings underscore the fact that key categories of whites are quite empathetic to the socioeconomic plight of their black counterparts. But to dismiss all of the empirical evidence detailed here is to miss the more revealing point: a significant number of whites harbor feelings of antipathy toward black Americans as a categorical group—feelings and sentiments that are openly and routinely expressed, as Paul Sniderman and Thomas Piazza rightly remind us. And where such prejudices are excited—by the press in particular—they constitute the critical linchpin in black office-seekers' success in garnering white votes. As Paul

Kleppner says of the 1983 Chicago mayoral contest, "[T]he existence of a racially charged contest helps explain why a biracial contest for mayor . . . had to become a battle. . . . No third parties, whether reporters or politicians, had to 'inject' race into the campaign; it was there, as it had been for nearly forty years, in the open, simply waiting to be mobilized at the polls."[12] Indeed, a fuller and empirically rigorous explanation of Kleppner's point can be found in the next chapter.

5

The Consequences of Cueing Subtle Appeals to Race

◆ ◆ ◆

What is a "subtle" campaign appeal? Subtlety in campaigns risks political ineffectiveness; only overt appeals are reliably heard.

— Abigail Thernstrom, *Whose Votes Count?*

Political unacceptability—the phrase is today's conventional wisdom regarding the failure of black office-seekers to attract widespread electoral support among white voters. "Plainly some whites may 'refuse' to vote for particular black candidates. Not because they are non-white but because they are politically unacceptable,"[1] is how Abigail Thernstrom puts it. "If Colin Powell clones ran in majority white districts in the South," she adds, "would they win? The answer is of course."[2] Her unmistakable point is this: blacks go down to electoral defeat because they are on the wrong side of the political fence. Rarely, of course, is race accorded similar import as an explanation for whites' often spirited resistance to the election of black office-seekers.

And if one suggests that racial campaign appeals hinder a black's ability to garner white support, this conjecture is hurriedly and brusquely dismissed. However, Leslie McLemore, a seasoned political analyst, had this to say about the 1982 U.S. congressional race in Mississippi between Robert Clark—a

black Democratic state representative—and his white adversary, Republican
Webb Franklin:

> Robert Clark has served 14 years in the Mississippi legislature. He was the
> first black elected since Reconstruction. He was chairman of the House
> Education Committee, a favorite of the speaker of the House, worked
> within the system. He was the anointed one, a kind of model of black can-
> didates in Mississippi. He had done all of the things you are supposed to do.
> But it came down to his race. . . . There was an organized attempt by Clark's
> opponent, Webb Franklin. But it was very subtle, not the usual Mississippi
> or South race-baiting demagogic campaign. His slogan was, "Webb
> Franklin stands for Mississippi tradition." *If you have any idea what Mississippi
> tradition is, then you get some notion of what he was doing* [emphasis added].[3]

On the contrary, declares Thernstrom, who presumes that "subtlety" does
not work in political campaigns. But subtle racial appeals, I have argued, do
carry electoral consequences. Indeed, Thomas Pettigrew has put the general
point well: "The race connection is in the listener's mind. It's already there
in white thinking, so you don't have to make it explicit."[4] It follows that
against the backdrop of a racially polarized campaign environment, the
"Webb Franklin stands for Mississippi tradition" slogan might well constitute
an alluring appeal that easily triggers discriminatory behavior among prejudiced segments of the white electorate.

In this chapter, I proffer empirical evidence that shows the political
effectiveness of subtle racial campaign appeals to whites.

Whites Say They Support Black Candidates, But Do They?

You will recollect that our social experiment involved the intentional experimental manipulation of campaign news stories that described a *nonpartisan*
election contest. The two mayoral candidates depicted in the articles were
Arthur Christopher, a local businessman with years of involvement in the
city's chamber of commerce, and his opponent, longtime city councilman
Gregory Hammond. As I noted in chapter 2, the news stories were identical
in all respects except for the mention of a campaign issue (the environment
as compared with affirmative action) and the racial identification of the
Hammond candidate.

After our study participants were carefully instructed to read a single campaign news story randomly assigned to them, they were asked to answer the following questions:

> We'd like to get your feelings toward the two candidates you just read about. We'll use something called the feeling thermometer, and here's how it works: We'd like you to rate each candidate using the feeling thermometer. Ratings between 50 degrees and 100 degrees mean that you feel favorable and warm toward that person. Ratings between 0 and 50 degrees mean that you don't care too much for that person. You rate the person at the 50-degree mark if you don't feel particularly warm or cold toward the person. How would you rate Arthur Christopher? How would you rate Gregory Hammond?[5]

Shown in table 5.1 are the mean thermometer ratings among the group of participants who read the campaign news stories that highlighted the environment as a central campaign theme. Recall that both articles described candidate Christopher as opposing stringent fuel-efficiency standards: he explains, "[T]he implementation of higher standards would cost jobs." On the other hand, Hammond, his mayoral opponent, favored tougher standards—"so long as they did not threaten jobs" (see figures 2.1 and 2.2).

What is clear from the data there is that Hammond was viewed more favorably among all of the study participants. For instance, the difference between the average candidate ratings among those assigned to read the same-race contest article is nearly 3 degrees—45.35 to 48.19. Among those who instead read the campaign story about the biracial contest—where Christopher is white and his counterpart, Hammond, is black—the difference in thermometer scores actually increased. The black Hammond candidate garnered a mean rating of 53.90, 8 degrees higher than Christopher, whose score was only 45.88. Finally, the difference in the ratings for both Hammond candidates—where they were described in identical terms, save for their racial identification—is nearly 6 degrees (48.90 degrees, as compared to 53.90 degrees).

At first glance, the feeling thermometer ratings highlighted in table 5.1 intimate that our white study participants were actually more receptive toward the Hammond candidate when the news story described him as black. But as the findings reported in table 5.2 indicate, those with college

TABLE 5.1. Candidate Evaluations Among Whites in Environment Story Experiment

Candidate	Same-Race Contest	Biracial Contest
Arthur Christopher	45.35	45.88
	(63)	(42)
Gregory Hammond	48.19	53.90
	(63)	(42)

Source: 1992 Biracial Campaign Election Study.

Note: Table entries are mean thermometer ratings where the range is zero to one-hundred. The larger the number, the more positive the evaluation of that candidate. The sample N's are noted in parentheses. In both campaign news stories, Christopher is white, while the race of the Hammond candidate was varied. In the same-race contest story, Hammond is white; in the biracial contest article, he is black.

TABLE 5.2. The Effect of Respondent-Level Attributes on Evaluations of Hammond Candidate, Environment Story Experiment

Independent Variable	When Hammond Candidate Is White[1]	When Hammond Candidate Is Black[2]
Education	-.36	-.16
	(2.91)	(3.29)
Age	2.44	.07
	(2.17)	(2.17)
Gender (Women)	4.50	7.29
	(6.00)	(5.87)
Ideology	3.89	-.71
	(2.51)	(2.29)
Constant	22.34	54.64★★★
	(16.87)	(14.28)
Adjusted R²	.02	-.06

Source: Analysis of 1992 Biracial Campaign Election Study.

Note: Table entries are ordinary least squares coefficients. The standard errors are noted in parentheses. The dependent variable is continuous and ranges from zero to one-hundred degrees.
[1]Minimum N=62.
[2]Minimum N=40.
★★★p ≤ .01, one-tailed test.

degrees were no more or less likely to view the Hammond candidate favorably—irrespective of his race. The same holds true for age, gender, and political orientation. Further, table 5.3 points out that whites' racial sentiments in fact exerted no influence on their evaluative judgments of either mayoral candidate. Whether Hammond was described as a white or black office-seeker, not one of the racial attitudinal measures achieved statistical significance.

To be sure, the evidence from the environment news story experiment suggests that the subtle racial campaign appeal—"Hammond . . . is seeking to become the city's first black mayor"—provoked no *perceptible* aversion among whites to support the black mayoral candidate depicted in our study. In and of themselves, the findings appear to support Thernstrom's presumption: that subtle racial cues are so vague that they miss their intended targets.

Yet there is one other equally plausible interpretation. The political effectiveness of "racial code" is related to whites' perceptions about the importance of race in the campaign. For instance, where whites feel threatened by the idea of a black candidate's bid for elected office coupled with the perception that that candidate has failed to allay their fears, racial campaign appeals are likely to strike their intended targets. As researchers Jack Citrin, Donald Green, and David Sears have observed, "Among factors that seem to enhance such sentiments [negative reactions to black candidates] are the size of the black population, the history of race relations in the community, and *the salience of racial issues in the campaign*" [emphasis added].[6] "The environment" is not an issue likely to rouse and mobilize racially prejudiced segments of the white electorate against black office-seekers who confront white political opponents. Interestingly, we are in a unique position to weigh the relative merits of differing opinions concerning the effectiveness of subtle appeals to whites: in our news story experiments we varied the campaign theme highlighted to one that is more racially charged.

First, the comparisons between the Christopher and Hammond feeling thermometers for those study participants randomly given the affirmative action news stories are shown in table 5.4. As indicated there, among those assigned the article about the same-race mayoral contest, the Christopher candidate garnered an average evaluative score of 49.10; Hammond, who is also white, received a rating of 53.75—a difference of almost 5 degrees. Keep in mind here that the news story described Christopher as an ardent oppo-

TABLE 5.3. The Effect of Whites' Racial Attitudes on Evaluations of Hammond Candidate, Environment Story Experiment

Independent Variable	When Hammond Candidate Is White[1]	When Hammond Candidate Is Black[2]
Attributional Blame Explanations:		
Blacks Have Less Inborn Ability to Learn	-.51	1.42
	(2.00)	(3.16)
Blacks Lack Motivation	1.60	6.24
	(3.16)	(4.10)
Blacks Prefer Welfare	-4.71	1.12
	(3.27)	(4.45)
Constant	22.34	54.64★★★
	(16.87)	(14.28)
Adjusted R²	.02	-.06
Situational Blame Explanations:		
Discrimination Hurts Blacks' Chances		
to Get Good Jobs	1.90	1.66
	(3.35)	(3.42)
Blacks Have Worse Jobs Because of		
Discrimination	-.81	.32
	(4.31)	(4.65)
Blacks Don't Have the Chance for Education		
to Rise out of Poverty	-1.87	-1.59
	(4.33)	(3.25)
Constant	22.34	54.64★★★
	(16.87)	(14.28)
Adjusted R²	.02	-.06

Source: Analysis of 1992 Biracial Campaign Election Study

Note: Table entries are ordinary least squares coefficients. The standard errors are noted in parentheses. The dependent variable is continuous and ranges from zero to one-hundred degrees. Control variables which are not shown here include education, age, gender, and political ideology.
[1]Minimum N=62.
[2]Minimum N=40.
★★★$p \leq .01$, one-tailed test.

TABLE 5.4. Candidate Evaluations among Whites in Affirmative Action Story Experiment

Candidate	Same-Race Contest	Biracial Contest
Arthur Christopher	49.10	49.27
	(52)	(56)
Gregory Hammond	53.75	52.09
	(52)	(56)

Source: 1992 Biracial Campaign Election Study.

Note: Table entries are mean thermometer ratings where the range is zero to one hundred. The larger the number, the more positive the evaluation of that candidate. The sample N's are noted in parentheses. Christopher is white in both news campaign stories, while the race of the Hammond candidate was varied. In the same-race contest story, Hammond is white; in the biracial article, he is black.

nent of affirmative action: he laments, "[Q]uotas are not the answer." In contrast, Hammond was portrayed as a *conditional* supporter of the policy: "I favor affirmative action programs as a remedy when there has been an identifiable history of discrimination by an employer," he reportedly remarked (see figures 2.3 and 2.4).

Interestingly, among whites who read the news story describing the biracial political contest, the difference in both candidates' thermometer ratings is a mere 1.82 degrees (49.27 as compared to 52.09). Though the black Hammond candidate gleaned a slightly higher evaluative appraisal than Christopher, the difference is not at all statistically significant. Meanwhile, the difference in both Hammond ratings—where, again, they were described in identical terms but for race—is not even 2 degrees (53.75 to 52.09 degrees).

Are the differences in whites' subjective appraisals of the Hammond candidate, in particular, conditioned by educational attainment, age, gender, or ideological orientation when his race was varied? To see whether this is so, consider the empirical findings presented in table 5.5. As indicated there, when the news story reported that the Hammond candidate was white, neither education, age, gender, nor political ideology was a significant determinant of whites' expressed evaluations. By stark contrast, when it was reported that Hammond was a black office-seeker, college-educated whites were likely to view him more favorably than their less well educated counterparts

TABLE 5.5. The Effect of Respondent-Level Attributes on Evaluations of Hammond Candidate, Affirmative Action Story Experiment

Independent Variable	When Hammond Candidate Is White[1]	When Hammond Candidate Is Black[2]
Education	2.24	4.50**
	(2.70)	(1.92)
Age	1.93	-3.71**
	(2.10)	(1.62)
Gender (Women)	4.34	10.20**
	(6.24)	(4.56)
Ideology	1.59	-2.29
	(2.53)	(1.73)
Constant	33.99***	-57.27***
	(12.89)	(11.44)
Adjusted R[2]	-.02	.22

Source: Analysis of 1992 Biracial Campaign Election Study.

Note: Table entries are ordinary least squares coefficients. The standard errors are noted in parentheses. The dependent variable is continuous and ranges from zero to one hundred.
[1]Minimum N=42.
[2]Minimum N=54.
**p≤.05, one-tailed test.
***p ≤.01, one-tailed test.

were. Older study participants, on the other hand, were less likely to proffer a positive assessment than younger whites were. And white women were likely to rate the black Hammond candidate more approvingly than were white men. Notably, though conservatives were less likely to express a positive appraisal of the black mayoral candidate than white liberals were, the coefficient failed to achieve statistical significance.

As for whether whites' appraisals of the black Hammond candidate were motivated by racial animus, the results shown in table 5.6 clearly point out that this was indeed the case. Although the Hammond candidate was described in precisely identical terms—but for the mention of his race— whites who read the biracial contest news story received the message of the "racial code" loud and clear. Specifically, those who concur with the view that blacks lack the motivation and willpower to pull themselves out of poverty were significantly more likely to proffer a negative opinion of the Hammond candidate—but only when the campaign story mentioned that

TABLE 5.6. The Effect of Whites' Racial Attitudes on Evaluations of Hammond Candidate, Affirmative Action Story Experiment

Independent Variable	When Hammond Candidate Is White[1]	When Hammond Candidate Is Black[2]
Attributional Blame Explanations:		
Blacks Have Less Inborn Ability to Learn	-1.42	.31
	(2.14)	(1.41)
Blacks Lack Motivation	1.86	-6.06***
	(4.21)	(2.44)
Blacks Prefer Welfare	.66	-6.31***
	(3.99)	(2.60)
Constant	33.37	94.41***
	(25.41)	(16.98)
Adjusted R^2	.03	.35
Situational Blame Explanations:		
Discrimination Hurts Blacks' Chances to Get		
Good Jobs	-4.42	2.97
	(4.22)	(3.80)
Blacks Have Worse Jobs Because of		
Discrimination	-3.12	4.85
	(3.85)	(3.86)
Blacks Don't Have the Chance for Education		
to Rise Out of Poverty	-4.19	-1.67
	(3.87)	(2.43)
Constant	67.60	49.58***
	(25.50)	(19.35)
Adjusted R^2	-.04	.23

Source: Analysis of 1992 Biracial Campaign Election Study.

Note: Table entries are ordinary least squares coefficients. The standard errors are noted in parentheses. The dependent variable is continuous and ranges from zero to one hundred. Control variables which are not shown here include education, age, gender, and political ideology.
[1]Minimum N=42.
[2]Minimum N=50.
***$p \leq .01$, one-tailed test.

he was black. Similarly, whites who endorse the notion that blacks exhibit more of a propensity to live off welfare than to work were more likely to express a disapproving view. Note also that where the black Hammond candidate is concerned, those racial sentiments that did achieve statistical significance are those involving "the character and capacities" of blacks as a categorical group. What is of greater import here is that although the white Hammond mayoral candidate is described in precisely identical terms as his black clone, he is unscathed by the subtle appeals to race.

What If the Election Were Held Today?

In addition to asking our study participants to rate each of the mayoral candidates using the feeling thermometer, we asked them to respond to the following question: "Based upon what you read, if the election were held today and you had to choose between the two candidates, who would you vote for (Arthur Christopher, Gregory Hammond) or are you undecided?"[7]

Table 5.7 shows the self-reported candidate preferences of whites assigned to read the news stories in which environmental policy was a central campaign theme. Among those given the article about the same-race political contest, Christopher and Hammond would receive 28 and 39 percent of the votes, respectively—"if the election were held today." Meanwhile, a third of the group (33 percent) declared themselves "undecided."

In contrast, among the group that read the story that varied the race of the Hammond candidate, Christopher garnered just 19 percent of the vote— a decline of some 9 percentage points. Meanwhile, 40 percent of whites selected Hammond, his black opponent; 40 percent categorized themselves as undecided. In the main, these findings are quite consistent with the feeling thermometer ratings (see table 5.1). That is, absent the perception of racial acerbity, subtle appeals appear not to have galvanized whites against the black office-seeker depicted in the environment story experiment.

As a point of comparison, the candidate preferences of whites who read the news stories regarding affirmative action are presented in table 5.8. As indicated there, among those who read the article describing the same-race contest, both Christopher and Hammond—each of whom is white—would receive 39 percent of the vote share "if the election were held today." Based on what they read, 78 percent expressed a preference for one of the two can-

TABLE 5.7. Candidate Preferences among Whites in Environment Story Experiment

Candidate	Same-Race Contest	Biracial Contest	Difference
Arthur Christopher	28%	19%	−9
Gregory Hammond	39	40	+1
Undecided	33	40	+7
Total	100%	100%	

Source: 1992 Biracial Campaign Election Study.

Note: In both campaign news stories, Christopher is white. The race of the Hammond candidate, however, was varied. In the same-race contest story, Hammond is white; in the biracial contest article, he is black.
N=111.

TABLE 5.8. Candidate Preferences among Whites in Affirmative Action Story Experiment

Candidate	Same-Race Contest	Biracial Contest	Difference
Arthur Christopher	39%	25%	−14
Gregory Hammond	39	26	−13
Undecided	22	49	+27
Total	100%	100%	

Source: 1992 Biracial Campaign Election Study.

Note: In both campaign news stories, Christopher is white. The race of the Hammond candidate, however, was varied. In the same-race contest story, Hammond is white; in the biracial contest article, he is black.
N=115.

didates. Less than a quarter of the study participants (22 percent) placed themselves in the "undecided" category.

Juxtaposed in the table are the expressed preferences of the experimental group that received the article that varied candidate Hammond's race. Here one will note a startling finding. When asked to indicate which candidate they preferred, only a quarter of the whites selected Christopher, the white candidate; as one can readily see, the difference in the percentage of respondents who preferred him across the two groups is 14 percentage points (39 as compared with 25 percent). On the other hand, the black Hammond candidate managed to attract only 26 percent of whites' support—13 points lower than his "white self" did. And among this group, just 51 percent indicated a preference for one of the two mayoral office-seekers.

What is particularly interesting is that rather than expressly stating an intention to vote against the black Hammond candidate, the subtle racial cues instead appeared to have triggered uneasiness and apprehension among whites. To put it differently, whites were unwilling to say that they would cast a ballot for either the white Christopher candidate *or* his black challenger. Indeed—and most surprising—the findings reveal a striking tendency on the part of whites simply to "vacate the field,"[8] that is, stampede toward the undecided category, as evidenced by the 49 percent who declared themselves "undecided." Observe that among those who read the biracial contest story, *the percentage of undecideds more than doubled.*

As for whether antiblack sentiments exerted an influence on whites' categorization of themselves as "undecided," table 5.9 highlights that the effect is both statistically significant and substantively revealing. For one, when whites endorse the view that the reason blacks have failed to reach parity with whites is because of "deficiencies in character and behavior," (attributional blame) they were *less* likely to be undecided when confronted with a seemingly uncomfortable electoral decision. By contrast, when our study participants endorse situational blame explanations (racial discrimination, lack of access to quality education, and opposition from whites) for racial inequality, they were *more* likely to declare themselves as "undecided."

In retrospect, the large percentage of "undecideds" is not at all surprising. Thomas Pettigrew, again, explains:

> If a black is running against a white, you look at survey data and you take the white "don't know" vote and simply add it to the white candidate's total. Ten times out of ten that's come within a couple of percentage points of what happens. It happened in Deukmejian-Bradley [1982]. An August Field poll showed Bradley ahead among white voters, with 43 percent to Deukmejian's 40 percent and 14 percent undecided. The final vote was 56 to 43 percent, in Deukmejian's favor. My rule of thumb would have predicted 54 and 43. . . . [T]he "don't knows" are not really "don't knows." They are already more or less in the white camp, and it's deceiving to think they really are "undecided" in the pure sense.[9]

TABLE 5.9. The Effect of Racial Attitudes on Whites' Self-Report of Being "Undecided," Affirmative Action Story Experiment

Independent Variable	Probit Coefficient
Education	-.08
	(.10)
Age	-.19
	(.17)
Gender	.65
	(.47)
Ideology	-.07
	(.17)
Attributional blame[a]	-.22***
	(.10)
Situational blame[b]	.44***
	(.15)
Intercept	-.10
	(1.37)
Chi-square/d.f.	53.65/47

Source: Analysis of 1992 Biracial Campaign Election Study.

Note: Table entries are probit coefficients. The standard errors are noted in parentheses.

***p $\leq$ .01, one-tailed test.

[a], [b] are summary indices based on the racial attitudinal survey items discussed in chapters 2, 4, and 5.

Indeed, further analysis of our "undecided" study participants indicates that they are not at all tolerant of black Americans as a categorical group. Fifty-seven percent of them *disagreed* that "blacks have worse jobs, housing, and education than whites because of racial discrimination." And 63 percent *do not accept* the argument that "blacks lack the chance for education it takes to rise out of poverty." These data lend empirical validity to the popular notion that the so-called hidden vote[10] really may end up in the column of the white candidate. Is it very realistic, then, to suppose that these individuals would support the black Hammond candidate once inside the confines of the voting booth?

If one were to employ "the Pettigrew rule of thumb" here, it is clear that if our black Hammond candidate went down to electoral defeat, racial animus on the part of whites, independent of other political factors, would play a deciding role. It should be emphasized, too, that because the social experiment enabled us to peer inside the "privacy" of the ballot, we have new insight into whites' openness toward the black Hammond candidate initially (as measured by the feeling thermometer ratings shown in tables 5.1 and 5.4). Whites' positive appraisals of the Hammond candidate had more to do with not wanting to appear as if they were discriminating on account of race than with a genuine willingness to support the office-seeker. But when actually faced with a choice, how whites responded to the black Hammond candidate is something else entirely—particularly when they perceived that race was a more salient and threatening issue.

It turns out, then, that Abigail Thernstrom's explanation of "political unacceptability" founders in light of the *empirical* investigation here. For against the backdrop of a racially charged election campaign, subtle racial appeals constitute a remarkably effective barrier to black officeholding. I have displayed the smoking gun—an obscure but nevertheless strong disinclination on the part of some whites to support the black Hammond candidate, who is of matched standing as a white candidate. *And I cannot overemphasize that the voting discrimination is discernible, specific, purposeful, and contemporary.* Indeed, "whites frequently act this way to the prospect of symbolic racial change—such as having a black mayor or governor—even when no objective racial threat seems to exist."[11]

What is more, our findings patently collide with the notion of "color-blindness" that many of our study participants—not unlike most white Americans—purportedly embrace. "Color should have NO bearing on qualifying a person for a job," wrote one respondent, while another commented, "The most qualified person should get the job regardless of race, color, or creed." As I have demonstrated, such pronouncements ring hollow under polarizing electoral conditions. In these instances, subtle racial appeals to whites *do* influence how black office-seekers are regarded.

And one cannot argue that whites' limited receptivity toward the black mayoral candidate in the affirmative action story experiment is due to his being "liberal in political orientation"; "lacking in qualifications and experience"; "inadequately appealing due to age, reputation or some other personal attribute." The campaign news stories expressly varied only the racial identification of the Hammond candidate. Whites' racial anxieties and fears surfaced only when it was reported that the Hammond candidate was black—even though he possessed identical credentials, personal background, and professional experience as his white clone.

I would also remind the reader of two other important points. First, because our study participants were randomly assigned to the experimental condition of reading one news story, as compared to another, *the resistance to supporting the black Hammond candidate in the affirmative action story experiment can be attributed to only a single causal explanation: the subtle appeal to race.* Second, because great care was taken "to anticipate and defend against" the weaknesses generally associated with experiments, the results here "can be safely generalized to populations of real interest."[12]

I have thus established a steadfast reluctance on the part of some whites to afford equal and fair consideration to a black office-seeker of matched standing as a white office-seeker, and this raises a serious set of concerns. For instance, where racial appeals—whether subtle or otherwise—impel whites to engage in discriminatory voting behavior, who would deny that black candidates' opportunity to compete for elective office has been significantly hampered? Are such prejudice and discrimination not barriers to attracting white political support—backing that is so necessary if blacks are to compete for statewide or federal office? Furthermore, for those running in predominantly white electoral settings where race is "one of the prime molders and shapers of political campaigns,"[13] how are black candidates to have an equal opportunity to compete for elected office, let alone win? And where the lack of equal electoral opportunity is found to exist, is an affirmative remedy not warranted?

In light of these fundamental questions that are raised by the arresting empirical evidence, I now wish to revisit the controversial public policy question of affirmative action, equal political opportunity, and federal minority voting rights.

III

AFFIRMATIVE ACTION AND EQUAL POLITICAL OPPORTUNITY REVISITED

◆ ◆ ◆

6

In Pursuit of a
Level Playing Field

◆ ◆ ◆

OK, you want to be colorblind, and that's fine. But we've got 30 percent of white people who won't vote for anybody black. How is that colorblind?
> —U.S. Congressman Melvin Watt of North Carolina,
> quoted in Nadine Cohodas, "Electing Minorities"

[T]he issue is whether a person like me, with my pigmentation, will have the opportunity to be elected to office. While Reconstruction used poll taxes to suppress blacks from voting, this [court litigation challenging the constitutionality of race-conscious districting] *is going in a more sophisticated way to silence us from having any meaningful role in the [political] process.*
> —U.S. Congressman Cleo Fields of Louisiana, quoted in
> Robert Stanton, "Minority Districts"

There is still a great deal of resistance to the election of black officials by whites in the country as a whole," one prominent scholar commented not long ago.[1] Indeed, the contemporary tendency of whites to discriminate against black political candidates on account of race shows how little *underlying* attitudes have changed despite the significant gains made possible by the Voting Rights Act. As we have seen, equal political opportunity cannot possibly exist where the subtle fanning of racial appeals impels racially biased behavior inside the confines of the voting booth. If "30 percent of white people won't vote for anybody black," how is this a level playing field? On this terribly important point, even Abigail Thernstrom agrees: "Evidence that political campaigns . . . have been 'characterized by overt or subtle racial appeals' is certainly pertinent to the question of equal electoral opportunity in a jurisdiction."[2] In fact, the direct and fresh empirical evidence presented in the previous chapter plainly underscores the startling relevance of her point.

It should not occasion surprise, then, that from 1878 to 1991, "the one constant in Louisiana politics"[3] was that no black in the state had been elected to the U.S. Congress. As surprising as it appears, since Louisiana gained admission to the Union in 1812, only three of the 184 members of the its congressional delegation have been black. Charles Nash, the first, served just one term, 1875–1877. And more than a century would pass before the two others—William J. Jefferson and Cleo Fields—were elected. What accounts for this 113-year gap?

To be sure, the answer lies in the state's well-documented and undisputed history of discriminatory voting practices and procedures: grandfather clauses; white primaries; "interpretation tests"; at-large elections.[4] Jewel L. Prestage and Carolyn Sue Williams, scholars of the South, summarize the prevailing view: "Louisiana's political environment has been hostile to the aspirations of blacks for equal political participation. Any alteration in this basic environment has been largely the result of 'outside interference' in the form of [f]ederal intervention."[5] Having employed such a plethora of schemes to resist the inclusion of blacks into the political process, Louisiana was —and remains—a "covered jurisdiction" under the Voting Rights Act. This means that the state is required to approve or "preclear" with the U.S. attorney general or the U.S. District Court for the District of Columbia any changes in its voting structures and procedures.

Following reapportionment in 1980, Louisiana went about the task of redrawing its electoral boundary lines to account for population shifts, as required by law. Rather interestingly, white state legislators met in the basement of the Capitol and enacted a congressional redistricting map with no legislative district in which blacks constituted a majority of the voters. In 1983, a panel of three federal judges invalidated the plan, finding that the legislature had "split every black precinct in Orleans Parish and created a district that resembled 'Donald Duck,'"[6] all to avoid having to create a predominantly black population district. Nonetheless, a subsequently adopted reapportionment map did include a majority-black district encompassing the geographically compact New Orleans area. It was this legislative district, where blacks comprised a numerical majority of voters, that sent William Jefferson, the state's first black representative since Reconstruction, to the U.S. Congress in 1991.

Indeed, it was the very kind of invidious practices employed by white Louisiana legislators during the 1980 reapportionment that led Congress to significantly amend the Voting Rights Act in 1982. The language, in part, now reads:

> No voting qualification or prerequisite to voting or standard, practice, or procedure shall be imposed or applied by any State . . . in a manner which results in a denial or abridgment of the right of any citizen of the United States to vote on account of race or color. . . .
>
> A violation . . . is established if, based on the totality of circumstances, it is shown that the political processes leading to nomination or election in the State . . . are not equally open to participation by members of a class of citizens . . . in that its members have less opportunity than other members of the electorate to participate in the political process and to elect representatives of their choice. The extent to which members of a protected class have been elected to office in the State . . . is one circumstance which may be considered: *Provided*, That nothing in this section establishes a right to have members of a protected class elected in numbers equal to their proportion in the population [original emphasis].

Subsequently, it has been the view of U.S. Justice Department officials (with a number of lower federal courts concurring) that where white bloc voting is present, the creation of majority-black legislative districts prevents the dilution of blacks' voting strength and at the same time facilitates black office-holding.[7] By carving out jurisdictions in which blacks comprise a majority of voters, then, the districts in the main increase the likelihood—but do not guarantee—that a black will be elected.[8]

Unquestionably, the policy helped usher in a significantly changed political landscape following the decennial census in 1990. And by no means is this an exaggeration. The number of blacks elected to the U.S. Congress, for example, increased from 26 to 39 in 1992, and to 41 in 1994. As the reader readily can see in table 6.1, were it not for predominantly black districts

TABLE 6.1. Congressional Districts Where Blacks Constituted a Majority of the Population, the 104th Congress (32)

District (Number)	Percent Black	Percent White	Representative
Alabama (7)	68%	32%	Earl F. Hilliard, D.
Florida (3)[a]	55	43	Corrine Brown, D.
Florida (17)	58	37	Carrie Meek, D.
Florida (23)	52	45	Alcee L. Hastings, D.
Georgia (2)	57	42	Sanford Bishop Jr., D.
Georgia (5)	62	36	John Lewis, D.
Georgia (11)[c]	64	34	Cynthia McKinney, D.
Illinois (1)	70	27	Bobby L. Rush, D.
Illinois (2)	68	27	Jesse Jackson Jr., D.[d]
Illinois (7)	66	29	Cardiss Collins, D.
Louisiana (2)	61	36	William J. Jefferson, D.
Louisiana (4)[c]	58	41	Cleo Fields, D.
Maryland (4)	58	33	Albert R. Wynn, D.
Maryland (7)	71	27	Kweisi Mfume, D.[e]
Michigan (14)	69	29	John Conyers Jr., D.
Michigan (15)	70	26	B. Rose Collins, D.

(continued)

(which, parenthetically, are some of the most integrated election districts in the country), fewer black lawmakers would have been sent to Congress. This is especially so of the South.

One of those riding the crest of political change in 1992 was Louisiana's Cleo Fields, the twenty-nine-year old state senator from Baton Rouge. With prodding from the Department of Justice, the state legislature interpreted the 1982 proviso to the Voting Rights Act to mean that "where a majority-black district could be created, one must be created."[9] Thus, to gain approval of its reapportionment plan, it carved out the district from which Fields was elected. Of seven congressional districts, Louisiana now had two that were predominantly black—the Second and the Fourth.[10] William Jefferson's geographically compact Second District in the New Orleans region was relatively easy to configure, as figure 6.1 highlights. By stark contrast, Fields's widely dispersed district, the "'Z' with drips" district, stretched from the northwestern city of Shreveport to his home base of Baton Rouge.[11]

But the Justice Department's policy of creating majority-black districts met with fierce criticism. Disputants charged that the districts convey the impression that voters were segregated on the basis of race, in violation of the

TABLE 6.1. (*continued*)

Mississippi (2)	63	37	Bennie Thompson, D.
Missouri (1)	52	46	William L. Clay, D.
New Jersey (10)	60	33	Donald M. Payne, D.
New York (6)	56	29	Floyd H. Flake, D.
New York (10)	61	27	Edolphus Towns, D.
New York (11)	74	19	Major R. Owens, D.
North Carolina (1)ᶠ	57	42	Eva M. Clayton, D.
North Carolina (12)ᶜ	57	42	Melvin Watt, D.
Ohio (11)	59	40	Louis Stokes, D.
Pennsylvania (1)	52	38	Thomas Foglietta, D.ᵍ
Pennsylvania (2)	62	35	Chaka Fattah, D.
South Carolina (6)	62	37	James E. Clyburn, D.
Tennessee (9)	59	40	Harold E. Ford, D.
Texas (18)ᶜ	51	38	Sheila Jackson-Lee, D.
Texas (30)ᶜ	50	38	Eddie B. Johnson, D.
Virginia (3)ᵇ	64	33	Robert C. Scott, D.

Source: Adapted from Philip D. Duncan, Christine C. Lawrence, and the Staff of *Congressional Quarterly, Politics in America 1996: The 104th Congress* (Washington: Congressional Quarterly Press, 1996).

ᵃ Corrine Brown's Third District was redrawn majority-white in 1996.
ᵇ This district—as of this writing—could be imperiled.
ᶜ In landmark rulings, the U.S. Supreme Court invalidated the Georgia district in 1995 and the North Carolina and Texas districts in 1996, declaring that they were created solely to guarantee that a black would be elected to Congress. In the aftermath of the 1996 rulings, the Court dismissed as moot the challenge to the Louisiana district. As of the 1996 Congressional elections, Sanford Bishop represents the redrawn majority-white Second District; Cynthia McKinney represents a reconfigured Fourth District; Texas Districts 18 and 30 were also redrawn majority-white.
ᵈ Served the remaining term of Representative Mel Reynolds who resigned in 1995.
ᵉ Retired from the House of Representatives in February 1996.
ᶠ The court challenge to the district was actually part of the case before the Supreme Court in 1996. The Court rejected the complaint because those individuals challenging the district no longer resided there.
ᵍ Representative Foglietta is white.

Equal Protection Clause of the Fourteenth Amendment. Furthermore, intentional racially configured voting districts, they allege, "raise the specter of racial quotas, deepening racial and ethnic cleavages, and minority political ghettos."[12] "These districts are reserved for black candidates; no white candidates need apply," one detractor argued.[13] Besides, wrote another, "[r]ace relations suffer when 'electoral remedies' favor one racial group."[14]

Such sentiments resonated with the U.S. Supreme Court when it ruled in 1993 that the shape of two majority-black congressional districts in North Carolina were suspiciously race-driven and subordinated traditional districting practices such as geographical compactness and contiguity, in particular.

FIGURE 6.1 Louisiana's Two Majority-Black Congressional Districts Drawn after the 1990 Census. *Source:* Adapted from *The Almanac of American Politics 1994.*

"So bizarre on its face" were the districts that it "rationally cannot be understood as anything other than an effort to segregate citizens into separate voting districts on the basis of race, the Court said."[15] The five-member conservative plurality, speaking through Justice Sandra Day O'Connor, further reasoned:

> Racial classifications of any sort pose the risk of lasting harm to our society. They reinforce the belief, held by too many for too much of our history, that individuals should be judged by the color of their skin. Racial classifications with respect to voting carry particular dangers. Racial gerrymandering, even for remedial purposes, may balkanize us into competing fac-

tions; [and] it threatens to carry us further from the goal of a political system in which race no longer matters.[16]

Indeed, O'Connor maintained that the state's First and Twelfth majority-black districts resembled "the most egregious racial gerrymanders of the past," and, accordingly, violated the constitutional rights of all voters to participate in a "color-blind" electoral process.[17] That said, North Carolina would have to demonstrate that its reapportionment plan was not drawn for an expressly racial purpose or, if so, that the plan was "narrowly tailored to further a compelling governmental interest."[18] Contorted majority-black electoral districts in Florida, Georgia, Louisiana, and Texas, all drawn after the 1990 census, were now open to legal challenge by disaffected whites. And challenge they did, filing lawsuits with vigor. Indeed, white complainants *claimed that race-based districting unfairly discriminated against them.*

Meanwhile, the Court plurality applied its reasoning in *Shaw v. Reno* two years later, when it invalidated Georgia's majority-black Eleventh District, represented by Cynthia McKinney, the state's first black congresswoman. The Court concluded that the state legislature's emphasis on race when it drew the boundary lines was "predominant" and thus unconstitutional.[19] In his majority opinion, Justice Anthony Kennedy insisted, "[J]ust as the state may not, absent extraordinary justification, segregate citizens on the basis of race in its public parks, buses, golf courses, beaches, and schools, the Government also may not separate its citizens into different voting districts on the basis of race.[20] What is more, the high Court made that perfectly clear by serving up a dramatic exclamation point a term later: in addition to striking down North Carolina's snake-shaped Twelfth District, represented by black congressman Mel Watt, the Court nullified two predominantly black districts in Texas—the Eighteenth and the Thirtieth—and dismissed as moot the challenge to Fields's "troubled" Fourth District in Louisiana.[21] "Government shouldn't encourage the assumption that people will vote or think according to skin color," was Justice O'Connor's nutshell opinion.[22]

Like it or not, however, a great number of us are left to contemplate the profound and vast implications of the Court's evisceration of race-based legislative districting. Undoubtedly, Justice John Paul Stevens grasped the dire, if not muddled, ramifications of the Court's 1996 rulings. In poignant, pointed language, he epitomized the concerns of many:

> The decisions issued . . . serve merely to reinforce my conviction that the Court has . . . struck out into a jurisprudential wilderness that . . . threatens to create harms more significant than any suffered by the individual plaintiffs challenging these districts. . . .
>
> I cannot profess to know how the Court's developing jurisprudence of racial gerrymandering will alter the political and racial landscape in this Nation—although it certainly will alter that landscape.[23]

Having treated *equal political opportunity for black office-seekers* as the principal focus of my inquiry, I would like, by way of conclusion, to offer a few final thoughts. From such a vantage point, it seems reasonable to speculate that, indeed, a tumultuous political landscape lies ahead.

The Diminution of Black Officeholding?

In the entire checkered history of this country, only nine blacks have ever won election to the U.S. Congress from districts where whites were overwhelmingly in the majority.[24] Following the 1990 reapportionment, black congresspersons were elected from Florida for the first time, and from Alabama, North Carolina, South Carolina, and Virginia for the first time in more than a century. Still, very few people seem to acknowledge that *all were sent to Congress from majority-black election districts*. As *New York Times* reporter Steven Holmes put it, "[T]he country will soon have to face a practical question that all those legislative contortions were intended to avoid: will whites vote for black candidates?"[25]

Critics of race-conscious districting habitually point to the fact that black Republicans Gary Franks of Connecticut and J. C. Watts of Oklahoma won election from majority-white congressional jurisdictions in 1990 and 1994, respectively; their electoral victories are demonstrable proof that whites *will* empower blacks at the federal level. But "general inferences drawn from a few easily recalled examples are notoriously hazardous guides to truth."[26] First, it should be noted—and I do so emphatically—that not only do Franks and Watts present a nonthreatening and noncontroversial demeanor to capture the support of white voters, but where race is concerned, their position is to reduce its salience to nothing. In other words, each is remarkably adept at exhibiting a "color-free" public and political face. Thus, where there are very few blacks actually living in one's congressional district, a Franks or Watts has a greater chance of getting elected, for there is no sizable black constituency to moderate the black candidate's stance on race. Indeed, critics of racial districting rarely, if at all, make mention of the almost indecipherable numbers of blacks who reside in Franks's legislative district—a mere 5 percent in 1996.[27] Or that blacks account for just 6 percent of the population in Watts's Fourth District.[28]

I cannot emphasize too strongly that if blacks comprised a higher ratio of the population, the race of the officeholder in either Franks's or Watts's district would be altogether different—especially against the backdrop of subtle and not-so-subtle campaign machinations. Why? "Empirical evidence indicates that the racial composition of the electorate overwhelms all other factors in determining the race of a district's representative."[29] For this reason, the greater a district's racial composition tips in blacks' favor, the more inclined whites are to project the racial fears and anxieties they hold about blacks as a group onto an individual black office-seeker. Andrew Hacker, author of *Two Nations: Black, White, Separate, Hostile, Unequal*, puts this central idea quite well: "Is this saying that even middle-age gentlemen like Douglas Wilder and David Dinkins rouse such anxieties? The answer is they can. This is what happens when voters choose to look at the black candidates not as individuals but, rather, to focus on a bid for racial power that the candidates are seen to represent."[30]

Empirical findings concerning patterns of racial residential segregation bear directly on this very point. Our study participants, recall, were asked a myriad of racial attitudinal questions in the face-to-face opinion survey (see chapter 2). Several of those questions inquired about the attractiveness of racially integrated neighborhoods. Specifically, we asked how "comfortable" they would be if their neighborhood came to resemble those depicted on the five housing cards shown in figure 6.2.

With the first card, respondents were asked to imagine that they resided in an all-white neighborhood—using the center home as their own. Indeed, this was not an unrealistic assumption for many of them. Then, they were presented the second card, depicting a neighborhood where one home was occupied by blacks, the other fourteen households by whites (scenario 2). If

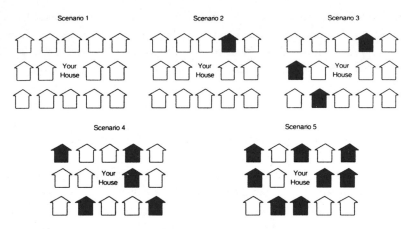

FIGURE 6.2 Neighborhood Diagrams Used For White Study Participants. *Source:* Reynolds Farley, Charlotte Steeh, Maria Krysan, Tara Jackson, and Keith Reeves, "Stereotypes and Segregation: Neighborhoods in the Detroit Area," *American Journal of Sociology* 100 (1994) 750–80.

a respondent indicated that she was "very comfortable" or "somewhat comfortable," she was shown scenarios with successively greater proportions of black households, until a housing card evoked an answer of "somewhat uncomfortable" or "very uncomfortable" or she came to the fifth scenario, an eight–households–black neighborhood.

An undeniable truth reverberates from the data displayed in figure 6.3: *as the proportion of black neighbors in the housing cards increased relative to whites, the "discomfort level" among our study participants heightened.* Just 35 percent of those surveyed in 1992, for instance, reported that they would feel comfortable residing in an eight–households–black, seven–households–white neighborhood. In addition, we took the first racially mixed scenario that elicited a response of "uncomfortable" and asked respondents if they would attempt to move away should their neighborhood come to have the racial composition pictured. Here again, the more black representation depicted on the housing cards, the greater the proportion of whites who said they would attempt to move. Indeed, 53 percent indicated they would try to move away from an eight–households–black, seven–households–white neighborhood. What is more, only 29 percent would ever be willing to move into such an area. "*The racial*

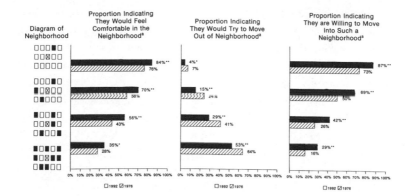

FIGURE 6.3 Attractiveness of Neighborhoods of Varying Racial Compositions for White Study Participants. Source: Reynolds Farley, Charlotte Steeh, Maria Krysan, Tara Jackson, and Keith Reeves, "Stereotypes and Segregation: Neighborhoods in the Detroit Area," *American Journal of Sociology* 100 (1994) 750–80. *Note*: Significance shown for change from 1976 to 1992; * p<.05; ** p<.01; the denominator for % is the total white population.

tolerance of whites has a limit, and neighborhoods with five or eight black households were not attractive. . . . White demand for housing in an area is clearly affected by its racial composition."[31]

Given their aversion to living in residential areas where blacks predominate, it is difficult to imagine whites supporting a black office seeker competing in such a context. Or to put it another way, if whites do not want to live among blacks, does it follow logically that they would vote for one who is *seen* as epitomizing a bid for racial power? To the criticism that majority-black districts amount to racial segregation, then, I am compelled to inquire, How is it that an election district where blacks constitute 60 percent of the residents offends whites' sensibilities, while a 91 percent majority-white district does not?[32]

Who, then, was the first political casualty of the Supreme Court's disparagement of race-based districting? None other than Cleo Fields. The political boundaries of his district were redrawn in 1996—for the fourth time. A U.S. district court imposed its own map, and it contained not two majority-black districts but one—William Jefferson's District 2. So Fields's

Fourth District was reshaped from predominantly black to majority-white, containing a mere 27 percent of black voters. This was a significant decrease from the 55 percent that helped facilitate his 1994 reelection.

There was a touch of irony in the fact that the U.S. district court's "new" District 4 contained white jurisdictions in which David Duke won a majority of the votes during his gubernatorial and U.S. senatorial campaigns in 1991 and 1992, respectively. "Five Supreme Court justices have done to [blacks] in Louisiana what no hooded Ku Klux Klan mobs were able to do in this decade—remove a [black] from Congress. The federal district court created a new district where David Duke, a former Klan leader, will have a far better chance of election than Cleo Fields," was the sober conclusion of one editorial.[33] Indeed, experts acknowledged it seemed more likely than not that Fields would go down to defeat. Thus, he declined to seek reelection in 1996. From my point of view, that race continues to loom large in Louisiana politics belies the notion that equal political opportunity exists for any black office-seeker. Is ensuring equal political treatment and opportunity not a "compelling governmental interest" and an extraordinary justification for race-based districting?

It is well-known that the "districting calculus" involves the complex and entangled interplay of race-neutral geographical and political considerations, chief among them the desire to protect incumbents. As Justice David Souter pointed out, "[D]istricting plans are integrated bundles of compromises, deals and principles."[34] Indeed, the Supreme Court has affirmed that the traditional practice of providing protection to incumbents constitutes a legitimate and reasonable districting criterion.[35] That said, what is fundamentally troubling is that the high Court's venture into the "jurisprudential wilderness" of legislative districting would technically prohibit the protection of black incumbents in Congress, all the while protecting white political incumbents as a matter of course. Such flagrant inequality is likely to—and should—trigger a political backlash among civil and voting rights advocates.

Suffice it to say that all this points to the almost certain diminution of black officeholding at the congressional, state, and local levels. But if the U.S. Supreme Court will not endorse the consideration of race in legislative districting, what remedial alternatives are there?

Policy Alternatives beyond Race-Conscious Districting?

Cynics who categorically impugn racial districting counter with this question: "Isn't the black community's interests better served if black voters are spread among many districts rather than concentrated in a few?"[36] In other words, numerically dispersing blacks across many electoral jurisdictions would both integrate them into the larger body politic and enable them to exert wider political influence over those elected (I presume white). In all candor, such reasoning not only smacks of paternalism but also devalues the inherent import black Americans may find in officeholding itself.

Justice Anthony Kennedy, for instance, holds the view that the proviso of the Voting Rights Act merely says blacks may vote, not that blacks should govern.[37] Surely he and his conservative colleagues on the Court do not actually mean to intimate that blacks have no place on the governing bodies throughout this country. What "lasting harm" does such a message, especially if enshrined in law, send to blacks—or other minorities, for that matter? I concur emphatically and fully with Tom McCain, one of the first blacks elected to political office in Edgefield County, South Carolina: "*There's an inherent value in officeholding that goes far beyond picking up the garbage. A race of people who are excluded from public office will always be second class.*[38] Thus, an equal opportunity to compete for—not necessarily win—elected office, not unlike voting or reporting for jury duty, affirms one's *full* citizenship in this country.

Still, the problem with "influence districts" is the presence of racial bloc voting on the part of whites. Consider, for instance, the 27 percent of black Louisianians who, as a result of the U.S. district court–imposed reapportionment plan, now find themselves isolated in an overwhelmingly white and undoubtedly hostile congressional district. Even local news media in the state maintain that the district is tailor-made for David Duke—or presumably someone of his ideological and political ilk. How does the election of such a representative serve the needs and interests of these blacks? In his or her voting record, or perhaps even his or her willingness to deliver rudimentary constituent services, would the representative not ignore the blacks residing in the district? Of greater significance, would Duke supporters and sympathizers even go along with the *open* courting of the black vote? And if

Duke—or a stand-in—were to write this black constituency off, would that not *reinforce* the racial divide in Louisiana electoral politics?

"Except that David Duke is such an extreme figure," the reader undoubtedly may object. "Couldn't the black community, in alliance with liberal-leaning whites, help defeat Duke and elect a more centrist candidate of its choice—white or black?" The answer, of course, is yes. "But where whites function as a cohesive district majority, a numerical racial minority simply cannot be influential."[39] If the truth must be told, even if blacks were able to help bring about the defeat of a white lawmaker who was indifferent or inattentive to their concerns, in the final analysis, "influence districts" could not be a remedy for the intractable problem of racial discrimination against black political aspirants.[40]

More interesting still, in the wake of the Supreme Court's flawed but significant opinions on race-based districting, is another policy idea that has gained increasing currency: "modified at-large" elections. For example, listen to the Center for Voting and Democracy's Robert Richie, writing in the *New York Times*:

> As the voters of Cambridge, Mass., Peoria, Ill., and several other American cities have discovered, there are ways to achieve this goal [fairer representation for all voters]: modified at-large voting systems such as preference voting and cumulative voting.
>
> Modified at-large systems are structured to allow more voters to elect candidates of choice without exercising any more voting power than other voters. Unlike race-conscious districts, they provide fair representation by allowing individual voters to define the representation they seek.[41]

Under a modified at-large election system, each voter casts as many ballots as seats to be filled and may do so in order of preference. A voter may give all her or his votes to a single candidate or divide them among several. It follows from this that blacks could strategically coalesce around a single candidate—white or black—and define for themselves the nature of the representation they seek. Professor Douglas Amy, a political scientist at Mount Holyoke College, counsels:

> [A modified at-large system] doesn't assume anything about how people want to be represented. It doesn't assume that blacks want to be represented by blacks or whites represented by whites. It simply allows individuals to

vote any way they feel depending on what criteria are important to them. Some may vote on the basis of race, some on the basis of gender, some on the basis of certain partisan considerations.[42]

Advocates of modified at-large elections cite yet one other prodigious advantage. Given that the geographical dispersion of blacks often hinders the creation of predominantly black election districts, dispersed yet politically cohesive black communities can still pick a candidate of their choice. Richard Engstrom, research professor of political science at the University of New Orleans, has observed that alternative approaches to the traditional "one person, one vote, winner-take-all" election system almost invariably lead to the election of black office-seekers.[43] "Cambridge, Massachusetts, for example, is 15 percent black and there has been a black representative on the city council since the '50s," says Rob Richie.[44]

Nonetheless, critics have sharply rebuffed the suggestion to adopt alternative voting schemes to enhance the political representation and electoral influence of blacks (and other minority groups). Despite their successful implementation by local jurisdictions across the country, many view modified at-large elections rather suspiciously. "The entire enterprise of trying to maximize racial strength in voting contexts is to me inherently divisive and counterproductive," argues Clint Bolick of the conservative Institute for Justice.[45] Indeed, many fear that if such reforms are implemented, they will ultimately lead to blacks' demanding legislative seats at the federal, state, and local levels in equal proportion to their numbers in the population; and perhaps other sectors of the electorate will even follow suit. In short, that adage about Pandora's box applies here especially: very few wish to see the specter of proportional representation unleashed.

The theoretical questions and merit about modified at-large schemes aside, all this begs one looming practical question: is the country likely to abandon its current system of voting? Not likely—if ever. For one, a 1967 federal statute requires the use of a single-member, "winner-take-all" voting system for congressional elections. Therefore, this law would have to be nullified—an improbable feat indeed, even for a lobby with considerable political, organizational, and financial muscle. "Legislators elected from . . . traditional districts are loath to change the rules that elected them," journalist Peter Applebome has mused.[46] Besides, when Congress approved a significantly amended Voting Rights Act in 1982, it made its views about proportional representation—and presumably any variant thereof—clear straightaway: "*Provided, That nothing in this section establishes a right to have members of a protected class elected in numbers equal to their proportion in the population.*"

Where the franchise is concerned, then, the political culture of the country remains profoundly opposed to "changing the rules of the game." The malevolent and highly successful 1993 campaign against President Clinton's nomination of Lani Guinier to be assistant attorney general in charge of the Civil Rights Division is an illustrative case in point. An impassioned champion of modified at-large election proposals, Guinier was relentlessly assailed by her detractors as "Clinton's Quota Queen." If confirmed as the nation's chief enforcer of civil rights, she would implement a "racial quota system for voting,"[47] or so the argument went. Indeed, Republican senator Orrin Hatch of Utah protested that Guinier's opinions "are frightening to many, even in the civil rights community."[48] Bending to the prevailing political sentiment, the president abandoned the nomination just a few months later. "I cannot fight a battle that I know is divisive . . . if I do not believe in the ground of the battle,"[49] an exasperated Clinton remarked.

My point here is not to suggest that modified at-large elections lack significant merit and promise but, rather, that they are so ardently opposed by the country's political leadership that as a public policy remedy, they are beset with colossal political and practical difficulties. The discrimination I seek to remedy, though, is "specific, identifiable and contemporary," and "there is a strong basis in evidence that remedial action [is] necessary."[50] So to critics, one related question is as pointed as ever: what would *you* suggest?

Given the limitations of the remedial alternatives I have already discussed, I come back to this conclusion: *race-conscious districting—albeit imperfect—is a demonstrably effective corrective action that brings about a level playing field for black office-seekers.* As I have shown, racial bloc voting among whites perniciously stacks the electoral deck against them. And until it diminishes, race-based districting is perhaps the only means of ensuring that blacks are afforded *an equal opportunity to compete for—not necessarily win—elected office.* This is neither a special privilege nor a means of insulating blacks from white electoral competition, as has been suggested.[51] Rather, it is a remedy to offset the voting discrimination against black candidates on account of race. As Justice Souter aptly put it, "[I]t is in theory and in fact impossible to apply

'traditional districting principles' in areas with substantial minority populations *without considering race*."[52]

I want to make clear that I neither disparage traditional districting criteria nor minimize the enormous complexity of this conundrum. But if the
notion of *equal political opportunity* is to hold continued legitimacy in this
country, there is really no other recourse but to reevaluate the permissibility
of race in the arena of legislative districting. This requires that the U.S.
Supreme Court, and indeed the nation, face up to the reality and seeming
intractability of race in American society—including our politics.

But critics of race-conscious districting assert that whites have moved
beyond voting against black candidates on account of race. Rather boastfully,
they point out that in 1996 five black members of Congress were returned to
office from redrawn majority-white jurisdictions. Therefore, it is no longer
necessary to draw legislative boundaries to enhance the election prospects of
black office-seekers. However the emphasis on electoral victory, it seems to
me, has obscured the fact that central to the success of Corrine Brown, Sanford Bishop, Cynthia McKinney, Sheila Jackson-Lee, and Eddie Bernice
Johnson was the incumbency status they held in their former majority-black
districts. Indeed, their incumbency status provided them with the benefit of
name recognition and a voting record. And most important, the power of
incumbency gave them great leverage in amassing formidable campaign war
chests. Table 6.2, for instance, shows how much campaign cash three of the
redistricted candidates raised as compared to their white challengers. Brown
out-raised her opponent by a startling $324,000; Bishop held more than a
2-to-1 advantage over his challenger, while McKinney amassed nearly $1
million to defeat a lawyer who had never held elected office. Therein, it
seems to me, lies the principal explanation for these instances of electoral tri-
umph: *the power of incumbency and the enormous leverage it affords.*

In addition, the basic fallacy in the pronouncements of critics is further
illustrated by figure 6.4, which highlights the degree of white support three
of the representatives garnered. Tellingly, Bishop attracted an estimated 36
percent of the vote share among whites in his largely agricultural district as
compared with Brown's 33 percent and McKinney's 31 percent; it is beyond
dispute that racially polarized voting loomed large in these elections. Given
the empirical findings detailed in earlier chapters, it is a reasonable inference
to conclude that some voting discrimination on account of race indeed took

TABLE 6.2. Redistricted Black Candidates' Fundraising Advantage, 1996 Congressional Elections

	Black Candidate's Amount	White Challenger's Amount	Difference
Corrine Brown,	$362,937.00	$ 38,413.00	+ $324,524.00
Sanford Bishop,	$751,143.00	$329,309.00	+ $421,834.00
Cynthia McKinney,	$997,369.00	$639,679.00	+ $357,690.00

Source: Federal Election Commission.

place. The truth is although the five redistricted black members of Congress won, they won despite that racial discrimination.

All of this, of course, raises a more central and penetrating question—one that disputants of race-conscious districting are reluctant to address: "Can a non-incumbent black candidate actually win in a majority-white southern congressional district?" Cynthia McKinney put the answer to that question in a sentence shortly after her 1996 victory: "The real test of whether majority-minority districts are still necessary will come from the minority candidates who vie for this seat after me."[53]

It is a laudable goal that "our political system ought to encourage people to look beyond race, to the qualities of individuals."[54] I find myself in full agreement with such sentiments—in an ideal world. But in contemporary America, the premise that "looking beyond race" will ameliorate racial prejudice and discrimination seems to me quite erroneous and misplaced. Interestingly, an episode involving General Colin Powell—four-star general, national security adviser, former chairman of the Joint Chiefs of Staff, mastermind of Operation Desert Storm, possible presidential contender—underscores this fundamental point. Frank Carlucci, national security adviser in the Reagan administration, sent Powell to speak with North Carolina senator Jesse Helms about a policy matter. Some time later, Senator Helms relayed to Carlucci that "he'd listened to that *black general* you sent up here."[55] Powell tells us, "See, now Jesse just don't know any other way to see folks. As cordial as Jesse and I are now . . . if you think Jesse can ever see me as anything other than a black general . . . [t]hen we'd have arrived. But we ain't arrived."[56]

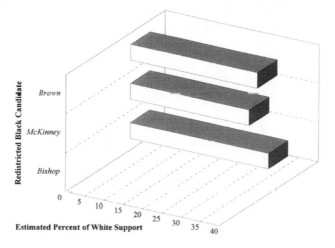

FIGURE 6.4   Redistricted Black Candidates and the Degree of White Support Garnered, 1996 Congressional Elections.

Nearly a century ago W. E. B. Du Bois admonished his fellow citizens to think clearly about the race question in this country: "Awful as race prejudice . . . and ignorance are, we can fight them if we frankly face them and dare name them and tell the truth; but if we continually dodge and cloud the issue, and say the half truth because the whole stings and shames; if we do this, we invite catastrophe."[57]

The last few years of polarizing litigation are evidence of the racial catastrophe Du Bois warned of. Facing up to an admitted race problem in this country is essential if we ever hope to arrive at the day when citizens are afforded an equal opportunity to realize their dreams and aspirations—without regard to race. Suffice it to say that one prediction is safe: if whites continue "voting their fears," we will never get there.

Appendix A

The Content
Analysis Study

◆ ◆ ◆

Coding procedures. Articles were coded paragraph by paragraph; articles, charts, maps, and headlines were treated as separate paragraphs. For each paragraph, coders first determined whether that paragraph used the terms "poll," "survey," or "percentage of (voters)" in the context of either a preelection poll or survey or an exit poll or survey. If so, they then recorded a series of additional variables pertaining to the precise nature of the poll reference. Similarly, coders determined whether each paragraph included a reference to race, blacks, whites, or any other racial or ethnic groups in connection with candidates, officials, celebrities, groups in the electorate, or race as a campaign issue. If so, they then recorded an additional series of variables relating to the precise context of the racial or ethnic reference. Finally, once all paragraphs for a given article were coded, a set of summary variables relating to the entire article was recorded. These variables included the general nature of the article (news, editorial, feature, etc.), the names of any candidates mentioned, the main substantive focus of the article, date of publication, page location, and other descriptive variables.

Variables. A subsample of 15 percent of the articles was double-coded in order to estimate the reliability of the measures. For categorical variables or ordinal and interval variables with very few values (i.e., less than four), a chance-corrected agreement coefficient (Scott 1955) was used to estimate item reliability; for continuous measures with ranges of five or more, an intercoder correlation was employed.

Appendix B

The 1992 Biracial Election Campaign Study

◆　◆　◆

Between April and July 1992, as part of the Detroit Area Study (DAS) at the University of Michigan, a representative cross section of 1,543 individuals (736 whites, 750 blacks, 57 others) residing throughout Wayne, Oakland, and Macomb Counties was interviewed face-to-face. The statistically random sample was drawn in a number of distinct stages.

First, the Detroit Tri-County area was divided into 9,000 segments, each comprising a census block or group of contiguous census blocks. A subset of these segments was randomly selected, and within each segment, each housing unit was listed. We then randomly selected those housing units in which face-to-face interviews were conducted. The total number of eligible individuals age twenty-one years and older residing in a given household was listed.

From this household listing we then randomly selected the respondent to be interviewed. If a person selected to be interviewed was not at home, repeated call-back visits were made in an attempt to reach him or her. In cases where an individual declined to be interviewed, we made several attempts to persuade that person to participate in the study. Of all the persons asked to participate in the 1992 Detroit Area Study, 1,543 agreed to be interviewed, for a response rate of 78 percent. Persons who resided in hospitals, educational and religious institutions, military facilities, hotels, or large rooming houses or who were homeless were excluded from the study.

The average interview lasted sixty-two minutes. Of the 1,543 interviews, 640 interviews were conducted by trained University of Michigan graduate students, 903 were conducted by professional interviewers from the Survey Research Center at the University of Michigan. And when it was feasible, we matched the race of the interviewer to the race of the respondent.

Given that the experimental phase of the project was administered by mail and that each of the original white respondents was interviewed face-to-face as part of the 1992 Detroit Area Study, it was necessary to employ a rigorous respondent verification procedure to ensure that the same individual who completed the mail questionnaire was, in fact, the *same* person who participated in the face-to-face survey. Hence, a "respondent match" variable was created comprising the key demographic characteristics of both respondent age and gender.

For example, the respondent whose gender in both the face-to-face and mail surveys was recorded as female but whose age differed—thirty-seven and fifty-six years, respectively—was denoted an "unmatched respondent" and excluded from any analysis. As an additional verification check, a respondent's age and gender across the two surveys were assessed in the presence of household composition data (i.e., all eligible respondents residing in the household, their gender and ages). Hence, the household composition information in the case of the female respondent who returned a mail questionnaire but whose age did not match that recorded in the face-to-face survey was used to validate her designation as a "non match" respondent. Of the 709 eligible respondents (Hispanics, deceased individuals, and those who moved were excluded from the experimental phase of the study), 365 returned completed questionnaires; of these 365 persons, this respondent verification procedure yielded a conservative 253 cases for analysis.

Finally, the demographic characteristics of our original probability sample indicate that our randomization procedures were carried out successfully. The original probability sample of 736 whites is nearly identical on key characteristics—education, age, gender, place of residence, partisanship, and ideology—as our experimental sample. Moreover, an analysis of variance (ANOVA) revealed no significant differences between assignment to one of the four experimental conditions and the core demographic characteristics. For instance, Republicans were no more likely to be assigned to receive the biracial affirmative action news story than the biracial environment article.

Similarly, less well educated respondents were no more likely to be assigned to receive the same-race environment campaign story than the one that described a contest between a black and white candidate.

TABLE A.1. Demographic and Political Profile Comparison of Original Probability and Experimental Samples

	Probability Sample (N=736)	Experimental Sample (N=253)
Age		
21–29 years	14%	13%
30–39	28	29
40–49	18	18
50–64	16	16
65–92	23	23
Average:	48 years	48 years
Gender		
Male	44%	40%
Female	56	60
Education		
High school or less	46%	46%
Some college	30	28
College graduate	13	13
Post-college	10	12
Place of residence		
Suburbs	87%	85%
Detroit city	13	15
Party identification		
Democrat	30%	27%
Independent	26	27
Republican	27	27
Other/no preference	17	18
Ideology		
Extreme liberal	2%	2%
Liberal	22	23
Moderate	41	38
Conservative	32	30
Extreme conservative	3	2

Source: 1992 Biracial Election Campaign Study.

Note: Percentages in some cases do not equal 100 due to missing data.

Appendix C

The Voting Rights Act

◆ ◆ ◆

Voting Rights Act of 1965

*(as amended through 1982 and as effective
on and after August 5, 1984)*

An Act to enforce the fifteenth amendment to the Constitution
of the United States, and for other purposes.
*Be it enacted by the Senate and House of Representatives of the
United States of America in Congress assembled,*
That this Act shall be known as the "Voting Rights Act of 1965."

Title I—Voting Rights

SEC. 2. (a) No voting qualification or prerequisite to voting or standard, practice, or procedure shall be imposed or applied by any State or political subdivision in a manner which results in a denial or abridgment of the right of any citizen of the United States to vote on account of race or color, or in contravention of the guarantees set forth in section 4(f)(2), as provided in subsection (b).

(b) A violation of subsection (a) is established if, based on the totality of circumstances, it is shown that the political processes leading to nomination or election in the State or political subdivision are not equally open to participation by members of a class of citizens protected by subsection (a) in that its members have less opportunity than other members of the electorate to participate in the political process and to elect representatives of their choice.

The extent to which members of a protected class have been elected to office in the State or political subdivision is one circumstance which may be considered: *Provided*, That nothing in this section establishes a right to have members of a protected class elected in numbers equal to their proportion in the population.

SEC. 3. (a) Whenever the Attorney General or an aggrieved person institutes a proceeding under any statute to enforce the voting guarantees of the fourteenth or fifteenth amendment in any State or political subdivision the court shall authorize the appointment of Federal examiners by the Director of the Office of Personnel Management in accordance with section 6 to serve for such period of time for such political subdivisions as the court shall determine is appropriate to enforce the voting guarantees of the fourteenth or fifteenth amendment (1) as part of any interlocutory order if the court determines that the appointment of such examiners is necessary to enforce such voting guarantees or (2) as part of any final judgment if the court finds that violations of the fourteenth or fifteenth amendment justifying equitable relief have occurred in such State or subdivision: *Provided*, That the court need not authorize the appointment of examiners if any incidents of denial or abridgment of the right to vote on account of race or color, or in contravention of the guarantees set forth in section 4(f)(2) (1) have been few in number and have been promptly and effectively corrected by State or local action, (2) the continuing effect of such incidents has been eliminated, and (3) there is no reasonable probability of their recurrence in the future.

(b) If in a proceeding instituted by the Attorney General or an aggrieved person under any statute to enforce the voting guarantees of the fourteenth or fifteenth amendment in any State or political subdivision the court finds that a test or device has been used for the purpose or with the effect of denying or abridging the right of any citizen of the United States to vote on account of race or color, or in contravention of the guarantees set forth in section 4(f)(2), it shall suspend the use of tests and devices in such State or political subdivisions as the court shall determine is appropriate and for such period as it deems necessary.

(c) If in any proceeding instituted by the Attorney General or an aggrieved person under any statute to enforce the voting guarantees of the fourteenth or fifteenth amendment in any State or political subdivision, the court finds that violations of the fourteenth or fifteenth amendment justifying equitable relief have occurred within the territory of such State or political subdivision, the court, in addition to such relief as it may grant, shall retain jurisdiction for such period as it may deem appropriate and during such period no voting qualification or prerequisite to voting, or standard, practice, or procedure with respect to voting different from that in force or effect at the time the proceeding was commenced shall be enforced unless and until the court finds that such qualification, prerequisite, standard, practice, or procedure does not have the purpose and will not have the effect of denying or abridging the right to vote on account of race or color, or in contravention of the guarantees set forth in section 4(f)(2): *Provided*, That such qualification, prerequisite, standard, practice, or procedure may be enforced if the qualification, prerequisite, standard, practice, or procedure has been submitted by the chief legal officer or other appropriate official of such State or subdivision to the Attorney General and the Attorney General has not interposed an objection within sixty days after such submission, except that neither the court's findings nor the Attorney General's failure to object shall bar a subsequent action to enjoin enforcement of such qualification, prerequisite, standard, practice, or procedure.

SEC. 4. (a)(1) To assure that the right of citizens of the United States to vote is not denied or abridged on account of race or color, no citizen shall be denied the right to vote in any Federal, State, or local election because of his failure to comply with any test or device in any State with respect to which the determinations have been made under the first two sentences of subsection (b) or in any political subdivision of such State (as such subdivision existed on the date such determinations were made with respect to such State), though such determinations were not made with respect to such subdivision as a separate unit, or in any political subdivision with respect to which such determinations have been made as a separate unit, unless the United States District Court for the District of Columbia issues a declaratory judgment under this section. No citizen shall be denied the right to vote in any Federal, State, or local election because of his failure to comply with any test or device in any State with respect to which the determinations have been made under the third sentence of subsection (b) of this section or in any political subdivision of such State (as such subdivision existed on the date such determinations were made with respect to such State), though such determinations were not made with respect to such subdivision as a separate unit, or in any political subdivision with respect to which such determinations have been made as a separate unit, unless the United States District Court for the District of Columbia issues a declaratory judgment under this section. A declaratory judgment under this section shall issue only if such court determines that during the ten years preceding the filing of the action, and during the pendency of such action—

(A) no such test or device has been used within such State or political subdivision for the purpose or with the effect of denying or abridging the right to vote on account of race or color or (in the case of a State or subdivision seeking a declaratory judgment under the second sentence of this subsection) in contravention of the guarantees of subsection (f)(2);

(B) no final judgment of any court of the United States, other than the denial of declaratory judgment under this section, has determined that denials or abridgments of the right to vote on account of race or color have occurred anywhere in the territory of such State or political subdivision or (in the case of a State or subdivision seeking a declaratory judgment under the second sentence of this subsection) that denials or abridgments of the right to vote in contravention of the guarantees of subsection (f)(2) have occurred anywhere in the territory of such State or subdivision and no consent decree, settlement, or agreement has been entered into resulting in any abandonment of a voting practice challenged on such grounds; and no declaratory judgment under this section shall be entered during the pendency of an action commenced before the filing of an action under this section and alleging such denials or abridgments of the right to vote;

(C) no Federal examiners under this Act have been assigned to such State or political subdivision;

(D) such State or political subdivision and all governmental units within its territory have complied with section 5 of this Act, including compliance with the requirement that no change covered by section 5 has been enforced without preclearance under section 5, and have repealed all changes covered by section 5 to which the Attorney General has successfully objected or as to which the United States District Court for the District of Columbia has denied a declaratory judgment;

(E) the Attorney General has not interposed any objection (that has not been overturned by a final judgment of a court) and no declaratory judgment has been denied under section 5, with respect to any submission by or on behalf of the plaintiff or any governmental unit within its territory under section 5, and no such submissions or declaratory judgment actions are pending; and

(F) such State or political subdivision and all governmental units within its territory—

(i) have eliminated voting procedures and methods of election which inhibit or dilute equal access to the electoral process;

(ii) have engaged in constructive efforts to eliminate intimidation and harassment of persons exercising rights protected under this Act; and

(iii) have engaged in other constructive efforts, such as expanded opportunity for convenient registration and voting for every person of voting age and the appointment of minority persons as election officials throughout the jurisdiction and at all stages of the election and registration process.

(2) To assist the court in determining whether to issue a declaratory judgment under this subsection, the plaintiff shall present evidence of minority participation, including evidence of the levels of minority group registration and voting, changes in such levels over time, and disparities between minority-group and non-minority-group participation.

(3) No declaratory judgment shall issue under this subsection with respect to such State or political subdivision if such plaintiff and governmental units within its territory have, during the period beginning ten years before the date of judgment is issued, engaged in violations of any provision of the Constitution or laws of the United States or any State or political subdivision with respect to discrimination in voting on account of race or color or (in the case of a State or subdivision seeking a declaratory judgment under the second sentence of this subsection) in contravention of the guarantees of subsection (f)(2) unless the plaintiff establishes that any such violations were trivial, were promptly corrected, and were not repeated.

(4) The State or political subdivision bringing such action shall publicize the intended commencement and any proposed settlement of such action in the media serving such State or political subdivision and in appropriate United States post offices. Any aggrieved party may as of right intervene at any stage in such action.

(5) An action pursuant to this subsection shall be heard and determined by a court of three judges in accordance with the provisions of section 2284

or title 28 of the United States Code and any appeal shall lie to the Supreme Court. The court shall retain jurisdiction of any action pursuant to this subsection for ten years after judgment and shall reopen the action upon motion of the Attorney General or any aggrieved person alleging that conduct has occurred which, had that conduct occurred during the ten-year periods referred to in this subsection, would have precluded the issuance of a declaratory judgment under this subsection. The court, upon such reopening, shall vacate the declaratory judgment issued under this section if, after the issuance of such declaratory judgment, a final judgment against the State or subdivision with respect to which such declaratory judgment was issued, or against any governmental unit within that State or subdivision, determines that denials or abridgments of the right to vote on account of race or color have occurred anywhere in the territory of such State or political subdivision or (in the case of a State or subdivision which sought a declaratory judgment under the second sentence of this subsection) that denials or abridgments of the right to vote in contravention of the guarantees of subsection (f)(2) have occurred anywhere in the territory of such State or subdivision, or if, after the issuance of such declaratory judgment, a consent decree, settlement, or agreement has been entered into resulting in any abandonment of a voting practice challenged on such grounds.

(6) If, after two years from the date of the filing of a declaratory judgment under this subsection, no date has been set for a hearing in such action, and that delay has not been the result of an avoidable delay on the part of counsel for any party, the chief judge of the United States District Court for the District of Columbia may request the Judicial Council for the Circuit of the District of Columbia to provide the necessary judicial resources to expedite any action filed under this section. If such resources are unavailable within the circuit, the chief judge shall file a certificate of necessity in accordance with section 292(d) of title 28 of the United States Code.

(7) The Congress shall reconsider the provisions of this section at the end of the fifteen-year period following the effective date of the amendments made by the Voting Rights Act Amendments of 1982.

(8) The provisions of this section shall expire at the end of the twenty-five year period following the effective date of the amendments made by the Voting Rights Act Amendments of 1982.

(9) Nothing in this section shall prohibit the Attorney General from

consenting to an entry of judgment if based upon a showing of objective and compelling evidence by the plaintiff, and upon investigation, he is satisfied that the State or political subdivision has complied with the requirements of section 4(a)(1). Any aggrieved party may as of right intervene at any stage in such action.

(b) The provisions of subsection (a) shall apply in any State or in any political subdivision of a State which (1) the Attorney General determines maintained on November 1, 1964, any test or device, and with respect to which (2) the Director of the Census determines that less than 50 per centum of the persons of voting age residing therein were registered on November 1, 1964, or that less than 50 per centum of such persons voted in the presidential election of November 1964. On and after August 6, 1970, in addition to any State or political subdivision of a State determined to be subject to subsection (a) pursuant to the previous sentence, the provisions of subsection (a) shall apply in any State or any political subdivision of a State which (i) the Attorney General determines maintained on November 1, 1968, any test or device, and with respect to which (ii) the Director of the Census determines that less than 50 per centum of the persons of voting age residing therein were registered on November 1, 1968, or that less than 50 per centum of such persons voted in the presidential election of November 1968.

On and after August 6, 1975, in addition to any State or political subdivision of a State determined to be subject to subsection (a) pursuant to the previous two sentences, the provisions of subsection (a) shall apply in any State or any political subdivision of a State which (i) the Attorney General determines maintained on November 1, 1972, any test or device, and with respect to which (ii) the Director of the Census determines that less than 50 per centum of the citizens of voting age were registered on November 1, 1972, or that less than 50 per centum of such persons voted in the presidential election of November 1972.

A determination or certification of the Attorney General or of the Director of the Census under this section or under section 6 or section 13 shall not be reviewable in any court and shall be effective upon publication in the Federal Register.

(c) The phrase "test or device" shall mean any requirement that a person as a prerequisite for voting or registration for voting (1) demonstrate the ability to read, write, understand, or interpret any matter, (2) demonstrate any educational achievement or his knowledge of any particular subject, (3) possess good moral character, or (4) prove his qualifications by the voucher of registered voters or members of any other class.

(d) For purposes of this section no State or political subdivision shall be determined to have engaged in the use of tests or devices for the purpose or with the effect of denying or abridging the right to vote on account of race or color, or in contravention of the guarantees set forth in section 4(f)(2) if (1) incidents of such use have been few in number and have been promptly and effectively corrected by State or local action, (2) the continuing effect of such incidents has been eliminated, and (3) there is no reasonable probability of their recurrence in the future.

(e)(1) Congress hereby declares that to secure the rights under the fourteenth amendment of persons educated in American-flag schools in which the predominant classroom language was other than English, it is necessary to prohibit the States from conditioning the right to vote of such persons on ability to read, write, understand, or interpret any matter in the English language.

(2) No person who demonstrates that he has successfully completed the sixth primary grade in a public school in, or a private school accredited by, any State or territory, the District of Columbia, or the Commonwealth of Puerto Rico in which the predominant classroom language was other than English, shall be denied the right to vote in any Federal, State, or local election because of his inability to read, write, understand, or interpret any matter in the English language, except that in States in which State law provides that a different level of education is presumptive of literacy, he shall demonstrate that he has successfully completed an equivalent level of education in a public school in, or a private school accredited by, any State or territory, the District of Columbia, or the Commonwealth of Puerto Rico in which the predominant classroom language was other than English.

(f)(1) The Congress finds that voting discrimination against citizens of language minorities is pervasive and national in scope. Such minority citizens are from environments in which the dominant language is other than English. In addition they have been denied equal educational opportunities by State and local governments, resulting in severe disabilities and continuing illiteracy in the English language. The Congress further finds that, where State and local officials conduct elections only in English, language minority citizens are excluded from participating in the electoral process. In many areas of the country, this exclusion is aggravated by acts of physical, economic, and political intimidation. The Congress declares that, in order to enforce the guarantees of the fourteenth and fifteenth amendments to the United States Constitution, it is necessary to eliminate such discrimination by prohibiting English-only elections, and by prescribing other remedial devices.

(2) No voting qualification or prerequisite to voting, or standard, practice, or procedure shall be imposed or applied by any State or political subdivision to deny or abridge the right of any citizen of the United States to vote because he is a member of a language minority group.

(3) In addition to the meaning given the term under section 4(c), the term "test or device" shall also mean any practice or requirement by which any State or political subdivision provided any registration or voting notices, forms, instructions, assistance, or other materials or information relating to the electoral process, including ballots, only in the English language, where the Director of the Census determines that more than five per centum of the citizens of voting age residing in such State or political subdivision are members of a single language minority. With respect to section 4(b), the term "test or device," as defined in this subsection, shall be employed only in making the determinations under the third sentence of that subsection.

(4) Whenever any State or political subdivision subject to the prohibitions of the second sentence of section 4(a) provides any registration or voting notices, forms, instructions, assistance, or other materials or information relating to the electoral process, including ballots, it shall provide them in the language of the applicable language minority group as well as in the English language: *Provided*, That where the language of the applicable minority group is oral or unwritten or in the case of Alaskan Natives and American Indians, if the predominant language is historically unwritten, the State or political subdivision is only required to furnish oral instructions, assistance, or other information relating to registration and voting.

SEC. 5. Whenever a State or political subdivision with respect to which the prohibitions set forth in section 4(a) based upon determinations made under the first sentence of section 4(b) are in effect shall enact or seek to administer any voting qualification or prerequisite to voting, or standard, practice, or procedure with respect to voting different from that in force or effect on November 1, 1964, or whenever a State or political subdivision with respect to which the prohibitions set forth in section 4(a) based upon determinations made under the second sentence of section 4(b) are in effect shall enact or seek to administer any voting qualification or prerequisite to voting, or standard, practice, or procedure with respect to voting different from that in force or effect on November 1, 1968, or whenever a State or political subdivision with respect to which the prohibitions set forth in section 4(a) based upon determinations made under the third sentence of section 4(b) are in effect shall enact or seek to administer any voting qualification or prerequisite to voting, or standard, practice, or procedure with respect to voting different from that in force or effect on November 1, 1972, such State or subdivision may institute an action in the United States District Court for the District of Columbia for a declaratory judgment that such qualification, prerequisite, standard, practice, or procedure does not have the purpose and will not have the effect of denying or abridging the right to vote on account of race or color, or in contravention of the guarantees set forth in section 4(f)(2), and unless and until the court enters such judgment no person shall be denied the right to vote for failure to comply with such qualification, prerequisite, standard, practice, or procedure: *Provided*, That such qualification, prerequisite, standard, practice, or procedure may be enforced without such proceeding if the qualification, prerequisite, standard, practice, or procedure has been submitted by the chief legal officer or other appropriate official of such State of subdivision to the Attorney General and the Attorney General has not interposed an objection within sixty days after such submission, or upon good cause shown, to facilitate an expedited approval within sixty days after such submission, the Attorney General has affirmatively indicated that such objection will not be made. Neither an affirmative indication by the Attorney General that no objection will be made, nor the Attorney General's failure to object, nor a declaratory judgment entered under this section shall bar a subsequent action to enjoin enforcement of such qualification, prerequisite, standard, practice, or procedure. In the event the Attorney General affirmatively indicates that no objection will be made within the sixty-day period following receipt of a submission, the Attorney General may reserve the right to reexamine the submission if additional information comes to his attention during the remainder of the sixty-day period which would otherwise require objection in accordance with this section. Any action under this section shall be heard and determined by a court of three judges in accordance with the provisions of section 2284 of title 28 of the United States Code and any appeal shall lie to the Supreme Court.

SEC. 6. Whenever (a) a court has authorized the appointment of examiners pursuant to the provisions of section 3(a), or (b) unless a declaratory judgment has been rendered under section 4(a), the Attorney General certifies with respect to any political subdivision named in, or included within the scope of, determinations made under section 4(b) that (1) he has received complaints in writing from twenty or more residents of such political subdivision alleging that they have been denied the right to vote under color of law on account of race or color, or in contravention of the guarantees set forth in section 4(f)(2), and that he believes such complaints to be meritorious, or (2) that in his judgment (considering, among other factors, whether the ratio of nonwhite persons to white persons registered to vote within such subdivision appears to him to be reasonably attributable to violations of the fourteenth or fifteenth amendment or whether substantial evidence exists that bona fide efforts are being made within such subdivision to comply with the fourteenth or fifteenth amendment), the appointment of examiners is otherwise necessary to enforce the guarantees of the fourteenth or fifteenth amendment, the Director of the Office of Personnel Management shall appoint as many examiners for such subdivision as the Director may deem appropriate to prepare and maintain lists of persons eligible to vote in Federal, State, and local elections. Such examiners, hearing officers provided for in section 9(a), and other persons deemed necessary by the Director of the Office of Personnel Management to carry out the provisions and purposes of this Act shall be appointed, compensated, and separated without regard to the provisions of any statute administered by the Director of the Office of Personnel Management, and service under this Act shall not be considered employment for the purposes of any statute administered by the Director of the Office of Personnel Management, except the provisions of section 9 of the Act of August 2, 1939, as amended (5 U.S.C. 7324), prohibiting partisan political activity: *Provided*, That the Director of the Office of Personnel Management is authorized, after consulting the head of the appropriate department or agency, to designate suitable persons in the official service of the United States, with their consent, to serve in these positions. Examiners and hearing officers shall have the power to administer oaths.

SEC. 7. (a) The examiners for each political subdivision shall, at such places as the Director of the Office of Personnel Management shall by regulation designate, examine applicants concerning their qualifications for voting. An application to an examiner shall be in such form as the Director of the Office of Personnel Management may require and shall contain allegations that the applicant is not otherwise registered to vote.

(b) Any person whom the examiner finds, in accordance with instructions received under section 9(b), to have the qualifications prescribed by State law not inconsistent with the Constitution and laws of the United States shall promptly be placed on a list of eligible voters. A challenge to such listing may be made in accordance with section 9(a) and shall not be the basis for a prosecution under section 12 of this Act. The examiner shall certify and transmit such list, and any supplements as appropriate, at least once a month, to the office of the appropriate election officials, with copies to the Attorney General and the attorney general of the State, and any such lists and supplements thereto transmitted during the month shall be available for public inspection on the last business day of the month and in any event not later than the forty-fifth day prior to any election. The appropriate State or local election official shall place such names on the official voting list. Any person whose name appears on the examiner's list shall be entitled and allowed to vote in the election district of his residence unless and until the appropriate election officials shall have been notified that such person has been removed from such list in accordance with subsection (d): *Provided*, That no person shall be entitled to vote in any election by virtue of this Act unless his name shall have been certified and transmitted on such a list to the offices of the appropriate election officials at least forty-five days prior to such election.

(c) The examiner shall issue to each person whose name appears on such a list a certificate evidencing his eligibility to vote.

(d) A person whose name appears on such a list shall be removed therefrom by an examiner if (1) such person has been successfully challenged in accordance with the procedure prescribed in section 9, or (2) he has been determined by an examiner to have lost his eligibility to vote under State law not inconsistent with the Constitution and the laws of the United States.

SEC. 8. Whenever an examiner is serving under this Act in any political subdivision, the Director of the Office of Personnel Management may assign, at the request of the Attorney General, one or more persons, who may be officers of the United States, (1) to enter and attend at any place for holding an election in such subdivision for the purpose of observing whether persons who are entitled to vote are being permitted to vote, and (2) to enter and attend at any place for tabulating the votes cast at any election held in such subdivision for the purpose of observing whether votes cast by persons entitled to vote are being properly tabulated. Such persons so assigned shall report to an examiner appointed for such political subdivision, to the Attorney General, and if the appointment of examiners has been authorized pursuant to section 3(a), to the court.

SEC. 9(a). Any challenge to a listing on an eligibility list prepared by an examiner shall be heard and determined by a hearing officer appointed by and responsible to the Director of the Office of Personnel Management and under such rules as the Director of the Office of Personnel Management shall by regulation prescribe. Such challenge shall be entertained only if filed at such office within the State as the Director of the Office of Personnel Management shall by regulation designate, and within ten days after the listing of the challenged person is made available for public inspection, and if supported by (1) the affidavits of at least two persons having personal knowledge of the facts constituting grounds for the challenge, and (2) a certification that a copy of the challenge and affidavits have been served by mail or in person upon the person challenged at his place of residence set out in the application. Such challenge shall be determined within fifteen days after it has been filed. A petition for review of the decision of the hearing office may be filed in the United States court of appeals for the circuit in which the person challenged resides within fifteen days after service of such decision by mail on the person petitioning for review but no decision of a hearing officer shall be reversed unless clearly erroneous. Any person listed shall be entitled and allowed to vote pending final determination by the hearing officer and by the court.

(b) The times, places, procedures, and form for application and listing pursuant to this Act and removals from the eligibility lists shall be prescribed by regulations promulgated by the Director of the Office of Personnel Management and the Director of the Office of Personnel Management shall, after consultation with the Attorney General, instruct examiners concerning applicable State law not inconsistent with the Constitution and laws of the United States with respect to (1) the qualifications required for listing, and (2) loss of eligibility to vote.

(c) Upon the request of the applicant or the challenger or on the Director's own motion the Director of the Office of Personnel Management shall have the power to require by subpoena the attendance and testimony of witnesses and the production of documentary evidence relating to any matter pending before it under the authority of this section. In case of contumacy or refusal to obey a subpoena, any district court of the United States or the United States court of any territory or possession, or the District Court of the United States for the District of Columbia, within the jurisdiction of which said person guilty of contumacy or refusal to obey is found or resides or is domiciled or transacts business, or has appointed an agent for receipt of service or process, upon application by the Attorney General of the United States shall have jurisdiction to issue to such person an order requiring such person to appear before the Director of the Office of Personnel Management or a hearing officer, there to produce pertinent, relevant, and nonpriviledged documentary evidence if so ordered, or there to give testimony touching the matter under investigation; and any failure to obey such order of the court may be punished by said court as a contempt thereof.

SEC. 10. (a) The Congress finds that the requirement of the payment of a poll tax as a precondition to voting (i) precludes persons of limited means from voting or imposes unreasonable financial hardship upon such persons as a precondition to their exercise of the franchise, (ii) does not bear a reasonable relationship to any legitimate State interest in the conduct of elections, and (iii) in some areas has the purpose or effect of denying persons the right to vote because of race or color. Upon the basis of these findings, Congress declares that the constitutional right of citizens to vote is denied or abridged in some areas by the requirement of the payment of a poll tax as a precondition to voting.

(b) In the exercise of the powers of Congress under section 5 of the fourteenth amendment, section 2 of the fifteenth amendment and section 2 of the twenty-fourth amendment, the Attorney General is authorized and directed to institute forthwith in the name of the United States such actions, including actions against States or political subdivisions, for declaratory judgment or injunctive relief against the enforcement of any requirement of the payment of a poll tax as a precondition to voting, or substitute therefor enacted after November 1, 1964, as will be necessary to implement the declaration of subsection (a) and the purpose of this section.

(c) The district courts of the United States shall have jurisdiction of such actions which shall be heard and determined by a court of three judges in accordance with the provisions of section 2284 of title 28 of the United States Code and any appeal shall lie to the Supreme Court. It shall be the duty of the judges designated to hear the case to assign the case for hearing at the earliest practicable date, to participate in the hearing and determination thereof, and to cause the case to be in every way expedited.

SEC. 11. (a) No person acting under color of law shall fail or refuse to permit any person to vote who is entitled to vote under any provision of this Act or is otherwise qualified to vote, or willfully fail or refuse to tabulate, count, and report such person's vote.

(b) No person, whether acting under color law or otherwise, shall intimidate, threaten, or coerce, or attempt to intimidate, threaten, or coerce any person for voting or attempting to vote, or intimidate, threaten, or coerce, or attempt to intimidate, threaten, or coerce, any person for urging or aiding any person to vote or attempt to vote, or intimidate, threaten, or coerce any person for exercising any powers or duties under section 3(a), 6, 8, 9, 10, or 12(e).

(c) Whoever knowingly or willfully gives false information as to his name, address, or period of residence in the voting district for the purpose of establishing his eligibility to register or vote, or conspires with another individual for the purpose of encouraging his false registration to vote or illegal voting, or pays or offers to pay or accepts payment either for registration to vote or for voting shall be fined not more than $10,000 or imprisoned not more than five years, or both: *Provided, however,* That this provision shall be applicable only to general, special, or primary elections held solely or in part for the purpose of selecting or electing any candidate for the office of President, Vice President, presidential elector, Member of the United States Senate, Member of the United States House of Representatives, Delegate from the District of Columbia, Guam, or the Virgin Islands, or Resident Commissioner of the Commonwealth of Puerto Rico.

(d) Whoever, in any matter within the jurisdiction of an examiner or hearing officer knowingly and willfully falsifies or conceals a material fact, or makes any false, fictitious, or fraudulent statements or representations, or makes or uses any false writing or document knowing the same to contain any false, fictitious, or fraudulent statement or entry, shall be fined not more than $10,000 or imprisoned not more than five years or both.

(e)(1) Whoever votes more than once in an election referred to in paragraph (2) shall be fined not more than $10,000 or imprisoned not more than five years, or both.

(2) The prohibition of this subsection applies with respect to any general, special, or primary election held solely or in part for the purpose of selecting or electing any candidate for the office of President, Vice President, presidential elector, Member of the United States Senate, Member of the United States House of Representatives, Delegate from the District of Columbia, Guam, or the Virgin Islands, or Resident Commissioner of the Commonwealth of Puerto Rico.

(3) As used in this subsection, the term "votes more than once" does not include the casting of any additional ballot if all prior ballots of that voter were invalidated, nor does it include the voting in two jurisdictions under section 202 of this Act, to the extent two ballots are not cast for an election to the same candidacy or office.

SEC. 12. (a) Whoever shall deprive or attempt to deprive any person of any right secured by section 2, 3, 4, 5, 7, or 10 or shall violate section 11(a), shall be fined not more than $5,000 or imprisoned not more than five years, or both.

(b) Whoever, within a year following an election in a political subdivision in which an examiner has been appointed (1) destroys, defaces, mutilates, or otherwise alters the marking of a paper ballot which has been cast in such election, or (2) alters any official record of voting in such election tabulated from a voting machine or otherwise, shall be fined not more than $5,000, or imprisoned not more than five years, or both.

(c) Whoever conspires to violate the provisions of subsection (a) or (b) of this section, or interferes with any right secured by section 2, 3, 4, 5, 7, 10, or 11(a) shall be fined not more than $5,000, or imprisoned not more than five years, or both.

(d) Whenever any person has engaged or there are reasonable grounds to believe that any person is about to engage in any act or practice prohibited by section 2, 3, 4, 5, 7, 10, 11, or subsection (b) of this section, the Attorney General may institute for the United States, or in the name of the United

States, an action for preventive relief, including an application for a temporary or permanent injunction, restraining order, or other order, and including an order directed to the State and State or local election officials to require them (1) to permit persons listed under this Act to vote and (2) to count such votes.

(e) Whenever in any political subdivision in which there are examiners appointed pursuant to this Act any persons allege to such an examiner within forty-eight hours after the closing of the polls and notwithstanding (1) their listing under this Act or registration by an appropriate election official and (2) their eligibility to vote, they have not been permitted to vote in such election, the examiner shall forthwith notify the Attorney General if such allegations in his opinion appear to be well founded. Upon receipt of such notification the Attorney General may forthwith file with the district court an application for an order providing for the marking, casting, and counting of the ballots of such persons and requiring the inclusion of their votes in the total vote before the results of such election shall be deemed final and any force or effect given thereto. The district court shall hear and determine such matters immediately after the filing of such application. The remedy provided in this subsection shall not preclude any remedy available under State or Federal law.

(f) The district courts of the United States shall have jurisdiction of proceedings instituted pursuant to this section and shall exercise the same without regard to whether a person asserting rights under the provisions of this Act shall have exhausted any administrative or other remedies that may be provided by law.

SEC. 13. Listing procedures shall be terminated in any political subdivision of any State (a) with respect to examiners appointed pursuant to clause (b) of section 6 whenever the Attorney General notifies the Director of the Office of Personnel Management, or whenever the District Court for the District of Columbia determines in an action for declamatory judgment brought by any political subdivision with respect to which the Director of the Census has determined that more than 50 per centum of the nonwhite persons of voting age residing therein are registered to vote, (1) that all persons listed by an examiner for such subdivision have been placed on the appropriate voting registration roll, and (2) that there is no longer reasonable cause to believe that persons will be deprived of or denied the right to vote on account of race or color, or in contravention of the guarantees set forth in section 4(f)(2) in such subdivision, and (b), with respect to examiners appointed pursuant to section 3(a), upon order of the authorizing court. A political subdivision may petition the Attorney General for the termination of listing procedures under clause (a) of this section, and may petition for Attorney General to request the Director of the Census to take such survey or census as may be appropriate for the making of the determination provided for in this section. The District Court for the District of Columbia shall have jurisdiction to require such survey or census to be made by the Director of the Census and it shall require him to do so if he deems the Attorney General's refusal to request such survey or census to be arbitrary or unreasonable.

SEC. 14. (a) All cases of criminal contempt arising under the provisions of this Act shall be governed by Section 151 of the Civil Rights Act of 1957 (42 U.S.C. 1995).

(b) No court other than the District Court for the District of Columbia or a court of appeals in any proceeding under section 9 shall have jurisdiction to issue any declaratory judgment pursuant to section 4 or section 5 or any restraining order or temporary or permanent injunction against the execution or enforcement of any provision of this Act or any action of any Federal officer or employee pursuant hereto.

(c)(1) The terms "vote" or "voting" shall include all action necessary to make a vote effective in any primary, special, or general election, including, but not limited to, registration, listing pursuant to this Act, or other action required by law prerequisite to voting, casting a ballot, and having such a ballot counted properly and included in the appropriate totals of votes cast with respect to candidates for public or party office and propositions for which votes are received in an election.

(2) The term "political subdivision" shall mean any county or parish, except that where registration for voting is not conducted under the supervision of a county or parish, the term shall include any other subdivision of a State which conducts registration for voting.

(3) The term "language minorities" or "language minority group" means persons who are American Indian, Asian American, Alaskan Natives or of Spanish heritage.

(d) In any action for a declaratory judgment brought pursuant to section

4 or section 5 of this Act, subpoenas for witnesses who are required to attend the District Court for the District of Columbia may be served in any judicial district of the United States: *Provided*, That no writ of subpoena shall issue for witnesses without the District of Columbia at a greater distance than one hundred miles from the place of holding court without permission of the District Court for the District of Columbia being first had upon proper application and cause shown.

(e) In any action or proceeding to enforce the voting guarantees of the fourteenth or fifteenth amendment, the court, in its discretion, may allow the prevailing party, other than the United States, a reasonable attorney's fee a part of the costs.

SEC. 15. Section 2004 of the Revised Status (42 U.S.C. 1971), as amended by section 131 of the Civil Rights Act of 1957 (71 Stat. 637), and amended by section 601 of the Civil Rights Act of 1960 (74 Stat. 90), and amended by section 101 of the Civil Rights Act of 1964 (78 Stat. 241), is further amended as follows:

(a) Delete the word "Federal" whenever it appears in subsections (a) and (c);

(b) Repeal subsection (f) and designate the present subsections (g) and (h) as (f) and (g), respectively.

SEC. 16. The Attorney General and the Secretary of Defense, jointly, shall make a full and complete study to determine whether, under the laws or practices of any State or States, there are preconditions to voting, which might tend to result in discrimination against citizens serving in the Armed Forces of the United States seeking to vote. Such officials shall, jointly, make a report to the Congress not later than June 30, 1966, containing the results of such study, together with a list of any States in which such preconditions exist, and shall include in such report such recommendations for legislation as they deem advisable to prevent discrimination in voting against citizens serving in the Armed Forces of the United States.

SEC. 17. Nothing in this Act shall be construed to deny, impair, or otherwise adversely affect the right to vote of any person registered to vote under the law of any State or political subdivision.

SEC. 18. There are hereby authorized to be appropriated such sums as are necessary to carry out the provisions of this Act.

SEC. 19. If any provision of this Act or the application thereof to any person or circumstances is held invalid, the remainder of the Act and the application of the provision to other persons not similarly situated or to other circumstances shall not be affected thereby.

Title II—Supplemental Provisions
Application of Prohibition to Other States

SEC. 201. (a) No citizen shall be denied, because of his failure to comply with any test or device, the right to vote in any Federal, State, or local election conducted in any State or political subdivision of a State.

(b) As used in this section, the.term "test or device" means any requirement that a person as a prerequisite for voting or registration for voting (1) demonstrate the ability to read, write, understand, or interpret any matter, (2) demonstrate any educational achievement or his knowledge of any particular subject, (3) possess good moral character, or (4) prove his qualifications by the voucher of registered voters or members of any other class.

Residency Requirements for Voting

SEC. 202. (a) The Congress hereby finds that the imposition and application of the durational residency requirement as a precondition to voting for the offices of President and Vice President, and the lack of sufficient opportunities for absentee registration and absentee balloting in presidential elections—

(1) denies or abridges the inherent constitutional right of citizens to vote for their President and Vice President;

(2) denies or abridges the inherent constitutional right of citizens to enjoy their free movement across State lines;

(3) denies or abridges the privileges and immunities guaranteed to the citizens of each State under article IV, section 2, clause 1, of the Constitution;

(4) in some instances has the impermissible purpose or effect of denying citizens the right to vote for such officers because of the way they may vote;

(5) has the effect of denying to citizens the equality of civil rights, and due process and equal protection of the laws that are guaranteed to them under the fourteenth amendment; and

(6) does not bear a reasonable relationship to any compelling State interest in the conduct of presidential elections.

(b) Upon the basis of these findings, Congress declares that in order to secure and protect the above-stated rights of citizens under the Constitution, to enable citizens to better obtain the enjoyment of such rights, and to enforce the guarantees of the fourteenth amendment, it is necessary (1) to completely abolish the durational residency requirement as a precondition to voting for President and Vice President, and (2) to establish nationwide, uniform standards relative to absentee registration and absentee balloting in presidential elections.

(c) No citizens of the United States who is otherwise qualified to vote in any election for President and Vice President shall be denied the right to vote for electors for President and Vice President, or for President and Vice President, in such election because of the failure of such citizen to comply with any durational residency requirement of such State or political subdivision; nor shall any citizen of the United States be denied the right to vote for electors for President and Vice President, or for President and Vice President, in such election because of the failure of such citizen to be physically present in such State or political subdivision at the time of such election, if such citizen shall have complied with the requirements prescribed by the law of such State or political subdivision providing for the casting of absentee ballots in such election.

(d) For the purposes of this section, each State shall provide by law for the registration or other means of qualification of all duly qualified residents of such State who apply, not later than thirty days immediately prior to any presidential election, for registration or qualification to vote for the choice of electors for President and Vice President or for President and Vice President in such election; and each State shall provide by law for the casting of absentee ballots for the choice of electors for President and Vice President, or for President and Vice President, by all duly qualified residents of such State who may be absent from their election district or unit in such State on the day such election is held and who have applied therefor not later than seven days immediately prior to such election and have returned such ballots to the appropriate election official of such State not later than the time of closing of the polls in such State on the day of such election.

(e) If any citizen of the United States who is otherwise qualified to vote in any State or political subdivision in any election for President and Vice President has begun residence in such State or political subdivision after the thirtieth day next preceding such election and, for that reason, does not satisfy the registration requirements of such State or political subdivision he shall be allowed to vote for the choice of electors for President and Vice President, or for President and Vice President, in such election, (1) in person in the State or political subdivision in which he resided immediately prior to his removal if he has satisfied, as of the date of his change of residence, the requirements to vote in that State or political subdivision, or (2) by absentee ballot in the State or political subdivision in which he resided immediately prior to his removal if he satisfies, but for his nonresident status and the reason for his absence, the requirements for absentee voting in that State or political subdivision.

(f) No citizen of the United States who is otherwise qualified to vote by absentee ballot in any State or political subdivision in any election for President and Vice President shall be denied the right to vote for the choice of electors for President and Vice President, or for President and Vice President, in such election because of any requirement of registration that does not include a provision for absentee registration.

(g) Nothing in this section shall prevent any State or political subdivision from adopting less restrictive voting practices than those that are prescribed herein.

(h) The term "State" as used in this section includes each of the several States and the District of Columbia.

(i) The provisions of section 11(c) shall apply to false registration, and other fraudulent acts and conspiracies, committed under this section.

Bilingual Election Requirements

SEC. 203. (a) The Congress finds that, through the use of various practices and procedures, citizens of language minorities have been effectively excluded from participation in the electoral process. Among other factors, the denial of the right to vote of such minority group citizens is ordinarily directly related to the unequal educational opportunities afforded them, resulting in high illiteracy and low voting participation. The Congress declares that, in order to enforce the guarantees of the fourteenth and fifteenth amendments to the

United States Constitution, it is necessary to eliminate such discrimination by prohibiting these practices, and by prescribing other remedial devices.

(b) Prior to August 6, 1992, no State or political subdivision shall provide registration or voting notices, forms, instructions, assistance, or other materials or information relating to the electoral process, including ballots, only in the English language if the Director of the Census determines (i) that more than 5 percent of the citizens of voting age of such State or political subdivision are members of a single language minority and (ii) that the illiteracy rate of such persons as a group is higher than the national illiteracy rate: *Provided*, That the prohibitions of this subsection shall not apply in any political subdivision which has less than five percent voting age citizens of each language minority which comprises over five percent of the statewide population of voting age citizens. For purposes of this subsection, illiteracy means the failure to complete the fifth primary grade. The determinations of the Director of the Census under this subsection shall be effective upon publication in the Federal Register and shall not be subject to review in any court.

[*Note: Section 4 of the Voting Rights Act Amendments of 1982 states: "Section 203(b) of the Voting Rights Act of 1965 is amended by striking out 'August 6, 1985' and inserting in lieu thereof 'August 6, 1992,' and the extension made by this section shall apply only to determinations made by the Director of the Census under clause (i) of section 203(b) for members of a single language minority who do not speak or understand English adequately enough to participate in the electoral process when such a determination can be made by the Director of the Census based on the 1980 and subsequent census data."*]

(c) Whenever any State or political subdivision subject to the prohibition of subsection (b) of this section provides any registration or voting notices, forms, instructions, assistance, or other material or information relating to the electoral process, including ballots, it shall provide them in the language of the applicable minority group as well as in the English language: *Provided*, That where the language of the applicable minority group is oral or unwritten or in the case of Alaskan Natives and American Indians, if the predominant language is historically unwritten, the State or political subdivision is only required to furnish oral instructions, assistance, or other information relating to registration and voting.

(d) Any State or political subdivision subject to the prohibition of subsection (b) of this section, which seeks to provide English-only registration or voting materials or information, including ballots, may file an action against the United States in the United States District Court for a declaratory judgment permitting such provision. The court shall grant the requested relief if it determines that the illiteracy rate of the applicable language minority group within the State or political subdivision is equal to or less than the national illiteracy rate.

(e) For purposes of this section, the term "language minorities" or "language minority group" means persons who are American Indian, Asian American, Alaskan Natives, or of Spanish heritage.

Judicial Relief

SEC. 204. Whenever the Attorney General has reason to believe that a State or political subdivision (a) has enacted or is seeking to administer any test or device as a prerequisite to voting in violation of the prohibition contained in section 201, or (b) undertakes to deny the right to vote in any election in violation of section 202, or 203, he may institute for the United States, or in the name of the United States, an action in a district court of the United States, in accordance with sections 1391 through 1393 of title 28, United States Code, for a restraining order, a preliminary or permanent injunction, or such other order as he deems appropriate. An action under this subsection shall be heard and determined by a court of three judges in accordance with the provisions of section 2284 of title 28 of the United States Code and any appeal shall be to the Supreme Court.

Penalty

SEC. 205. Whoever shall deprive or attempt to deprive any person of any right secured by section 201, 202, or 203 of this title shall be fined not more than $5,000, or imprisoned not more than five years, or both.

Separability

SEC. 206. If any provision of this Act or the application of any provision thereof to any person or circumstance is judicially determined to be invalid, the remainder of this Act or the application of such provision to other persons or circumstances shall not be affected by such determination.

SEC. 207. (a) Congress hereby directs the Director of the Census forthwith to conduct a survey to compile registration and voting statistics: (i) in every State or political subdivision with respect to which the prohibitions of section 4(a) of the Voting Rights Act of 1965 are in effect, for every statewide general election for Members of the United States House of Representatives after January 1, 1974; and (ii) in every State or political subdivision for any election designated by the United States Commission on Civil Rights. Such surveys shall only include a count of citizens of voting age, race or color, and national origin, and a determination of the extent to which such persons are registered to vote and have voted in the elections surveyed.

(b) In any survey under subsection (a) of this section no person shall be compelled to disclose his race, color, national origin, political party affiliation, or how he voted (or the reasons therefor), now shall any penalty be imposed for his failure or refusal to make such disclosures. Every person interrogated orally, by written survey or questionnaire, or by any other means with respect to such information shall be fully advised of his right to fail or refuse to furnish such information.

(c) The Director of the Census shall, at the earliest practicable time, report to the Congress the results of every survey conducted pursuant to the provisions of subsection (a) of this section.

(d) The provisions of section 9 and chapter 7 of title 13 of the United States Code shall apply to any survey, collection, or compilation of registration and voting statistics carried out under subsection (a) of this section.

Voting Assistance

SEC. 208. Any voter who requires assistance to vote by reason of blindness, disability, or inability to read or write may be given assistance by a person of the voter's choice, other than the voter's employer or agent of that employer or officer or agent of the voter's union.

Title III—Eighteen-Year-Old Voting Age

Enforcement of Twenty-Sixth Amendment

SEC. 301. (a)(1) The Attorney General is directed to institute, in the name of the United States, such actions against States or political subdivisions, including actions for injunctive relief, as he may determine to be necessary to implement the twenty-sixth article of amendment to the Constitution of the United States.

(2) The district courts of the United States shall have jurisdiction of proceedings instituted under this title, which shall be heard and determined by a court of three judges in accordance with section 2284 of title 28 of the United States Code, and any appeal shall lie to the Supreme Court. It shall be the duty of the judges designated to hear the case to assign the case for hearing and determination thereof, and to cause the case to be in every way expedited.

(b) Whoever shall deny or attempt to deny any person of any right secured by the twenty-sixth article of amendment to the Constitution of the United States shall be fined not more than $5,000 or imprisoned not more than five years, or both.

Definition

SEC. 302. As used in this title, the term "State" includes the District of Columbia.

[*Note: As enacted, the Voting Rights Act, in Sections 3, 6, 7, 8, 9, and 13, contains references to the United States Civil Service Commission. Because the functions of the Civil Service Commission have been transferred to the Director of the Office of Personnel Management, references in the Act to the Commission have been changed to references to the Director.*]

Notes

♦ ♦ ♦

Foreword

1. A full explanation of the precept whereby blacks were assumed to be inferior and the consequences of that precept are developed in extensive detail in Higginbotham 1996b.

2. Ibid, p. 17.

3. See Higginbotham, Clarick, and David 1994, p. 1593.

4. *Shaw v. Reno,* 113 S. Ct. 2816, 2834 (1993) (Justice White, dissenting).

5. *Hays v. Louisiana III,* CV 92-1522, 95-1241 (W.D.La. 1996). *Hays v. Louisiana* was litigated three times in the federal district court and was heard by the Supreme Court in 1995.

6. See Higginbotham 1996a, p. 23.

Introduction

1. These data are from a March 23–24, 1995, national telephone poll conducted by Princeton Survey Research Associates for *Newsweek.* 752 adults were interviewed, and the margin of error is +/- 4 percentage points. The actual wording of the question is as follows: "Do you believe that, because of past discrimination against black people, qualified blacks should receive preference over equally qualified whites in such matters as getting into college and getting jobs, or not?" Personal communication. See also Fineman 1995, pp. 22–25.

2. *American National Election Studies, 1948–1994.* The wording of the question is as follows: "Some people feel that the government in Washington should make every effort to improve the social and economic position of blacks. Others feel that the government should not make any special effort to help blacks because they should help themselves."

3. Morin 1995, pp. A1, A26–27.

4. The U.S. Commission on Civil Rights defines affirmative action as: "[A]

contemporary term that encompasses any measure, beyond simple termination of a discriminatory practice, that permits the consideration of race, national origin, sex, or disability, along with other criteria, and which is *adopted to provide opportunities to a class of qualified individuals who have either historically or actually been denied those opportunities and/or to prevent the recurrence of discrimination in the future*" (U.S. Commission on Civil Rights 1981; U.S. Commission on Civil Rights 1977; emphasis added).

5. It should be pointed out, too, that Johnson's Howard University commencement address was well received by the civil rights leadership.

6. Myrdal 1944, p. lxix.

7. The Voting Rights Act of 1965 defined a voting prerequisite as a "test or device" requiring an individual to: (a) demonstrate the ability to read, write, understand, or interpret any matter, (b) demonstrate any educational achievement or his knowledge of any particular subject, (c) possess good moral character, or (4) prove his qualifications by the voucher of registered voters or members of any other class. See Grofman and Davidson 1992, p. 18, N. 43.

8. See, for instance, Thernstrom 1979; Butler 1984; Schuck 1987; Thernstrom 1987; Karlan and McCrary 1988; McDonald 1989; Parker 1990; Grofman and Davidson 1992; Grofman, Handley, and Niemi 1992; Swain 1993; Guinier 1994; Davidson and Grofman 1994; Cohodas 1994; Reeves and Cohodas 1995a; Reeves and Cohodas 1995b; Thernstrom 1995. And for an excellent overview and discussion of the issues and challenges confronting minority-elected officeholders at present, see Feeney and McGonigle 1994.

9. Brischetto et al. 1994, p. 242: "One of the first successful voting cases brought by MALDEF [the Mexican American Legal Defense and Education Fund] was *Garza v. Smith* (1970). This action challenged Texas election laws that enabled voting officials to assist physically handicapped voters but did not permit assistance to voters who were not proficient in English. The argument foreshadowed the broadening of [S]ection 5 coverage to Texas five years later. In its 1975 extension of the act, Congress concluded that 'where State and local officials conduct elections only in English, language minority citizens are excluded from participating in the electoral process.' Congress therefore brought under [S]ection 5 coverage some of those states and counties that had historically failed to provide multilingual election materials."

10. Cohodas 1994, p. 699.

11. Thernstrom 1987, pp. 3–4. Others, however, take an entirely different interpretation of the legislation's intent. For instance, see Grofman, Handley, and Niemi 1992, pp. 129–30.

12. Schuck 1987, p. 53.

13. Thernstrom 1987, pp. 1–10.

14. Cain 1992, p. 261: "The most common objection to the evolution of voting rights laws and enforcement is that it has bestowed special representation advantages upon some racial and ethnic groups but not others and has pulled the United States back from its cherished ideal of a color-blind society."

15. See, principally, Schuman, Steeh, and Bobo 1985.

16. Thernstrom 1995, p. A15.

17. Tom Bradley was first elected in 1973 and served until June 1993. Ernest Morial won the New Orleans mayoralty in 1977 with 19 percent of the white vote. Garnering no more than 12 percent of the vote share among white Chicagoans, Harold Washington was elected in 1983; he won a second term in 1987 but died a few weeks after being sworn in. And in a city where Democrats outnumber Republicans 5 to 1, Dinkins won the New York mayoralty by just two percentage points, capturing just 31 percent of the white vote in 1989; he lost his 1993 bid for reelection. Norman Rice was elected in 1989. Having gained the support of 42 percent of whites, Ron Kirk became Dallas's first black mayor in 1995. It should be emphasized that it is very difficult for black candidates to be elected outside majority-black jurisdictions, despite these well-publicized cases. See Grofman, Handley, and Niemi 1992, pp. 134–37; Lublin 1995, pp. 111–25.

18. Exit polls showed that Wilder managed to garner 39 percent of the white vote.

19. Moseley-Braun won 48 percent of the white vote and a 58 percent vote share among women, according to exit polls.

20. Pildes 1995, p. C1.

21. Ibid.

22. Grofman, Handley, and Niemi 1992, pp. 134–37.

23. The Fifteenth Amendment reads as follows: "Section 1. The right of citizens of the United States to vote shall not be denied or abridged by the United States or by any State on account of race, color, or previous condition of servitude; Section 2. The Congress shall have power to enforce this article by appropriate legislation."

24. Joint Center for Political and Economic Studies 1993.

25. Ibid.

Chapter 1

1. See, for example, Bartels 1988; Goldenberg and Traugott 1984; Kinder and Sears 1985; Salmore and Salmore 1989.

2. Becker, McCombs, and McLeod 1975; Goldenberg and Traugott 1984; Salmore and Salmore 1989.

3. Goldenberg and Traugott 1984; Jamieson 1992; Kleppner 1985.

4. Becker and Heaton 1967; Cavanagh 1983; Edsall with Edsall 1992; Hacker 1995; Huckfeldt and Kohfeld 1989; Jamieson 1992; Kinder and Sanders 1996; Kleppner 1985; Kuzenski, Bullock, and Gaddie 1995; Metz and Tate 1995; Pettigrew 1972; Pettigrew and Alston 1988; Pinderhughes 1987; Reeves 1994b; Rose 1992.

5. Horton's two companions were Alvin Wideman and Roosevelt Pickett, their victim seventeen-year-old Joey Fournier. The three men stabbed Fournier nineteen times, leaving his body in a trash barrel. For a more detailed description of the Horton case, see Bidinotto 1988, pp. 57–63.

6. The national Democratic Party's platform read, "Recognition of the consti-tutional and human rights of prisoners; realistic therapeutic, vocational, wage-earn-ing, education, alcoholism, and drug treatment programs . . . emergency, educational and work-release furlough programs as an available technique." See Johnson 1978, p. 809.

7. Bidinotto 1988; Edsall with Edsall 1992, pp. 222–25.

8. Edsall with Edsall, pp. 222–25.

9. Ibid. The Edsalls report that Atwater delivered these comments to a group of southern Republicans in Atlanta on July 9, 1988.

10. Irish 1942, p. 80.

11. Kathleen Hall Jamieson notes that though the first Willie Horton ad wasn't unveiled until the second week in September, Bush began telling the story on the campaign trail as early as June 1988. In early October, the National Security Political Action Committee (NSPAC) released its "revolving door" ad to dramatize the seem-ing laxness of Massachusetts's furlough system under Governor Dukakis. In her dis-cussion of the inaccuracies in the "revolving door" ad, Professor Jamieson explains that the ad inferred that Governor Dukakis furloughed some 268 first-degree mur-derers to rape and kidnap. Jamieson 1992, pp. 20–21: "But many unparoleable first-degree murderers did not escape. Of the 268 furloughed convicts who jumped fur-lough during Dukakis's first two terms, only four had ever been convicted first-degree murderers not eligible for parole. Of those four not 'many' but one went on to kidnap and rape. That one was Willie Horton. By flashing '268 escaped' on the screen as the announcer speaks of 'many first-degree murderers,' the ad invites the false inference that 268 murderers jumped furlough to rape and kidnap again. Again, the single indi-vidual who fits this description is Horton. Finally, the actual number who were more than four hours late in returning from furlough during Dukakis' two and a half terms was not 268 but 275. In Dukakis' first two terms, 268 escapes were made by the 11,497 individuals who were given a total of 67,378 furloughs. In the ten-year period encompassing his completed terms and the first two years of his third term (1987–88), 275 of 76,455 furloughs resulted in escape." An important point should be raised here. The *precise causal impact* of such racially explicit campaign information on voters' evaluations of and preferences for Bush and Dukakis remains speculative. For an interesting discussion of one of the Horton ads in an experimental study, see Mendelberg 1992.

12. Jamieson 1992, p. 24.

13. Edsall with Edsall, pp. 222–25.

14. Ibid., p. 224.

15. Jamieson 1992, pp. 94–100.

16. See Martin 1991; Jamieson 1992; Kennedy School of Government Case Study 1992.

17. Jamieson 1992, p. 97.

18. Ibid., pp. 99–100.

19. Martin 1991. Gantt, garnering 36 percent of white support, lost to Helms in their 1996 rematch.

20. Jamieson 1992, p. 84.

21. Kleppner reports that the Republican strategist's comment was reported in a *Chicago Tribune* article dated March 27, 1983. See Kleppner 1985, p. 210.

22. Ibid., p. 207.

23. Washington defeated Epton by a margin of 46,250 votes out of 1.29 million ballots cast; he managed to garner only 12.3 percent of the white vote, as compared with Epton's 87.6 percent. See Kleppner 1985, pp. 216—39.

24. Kinder and Mendelberg 1991.

25. Kleppner 1985, p. 250.

26. Huckfeldt and Kohfeld 1989, p. 44.

27. Luebke quoted in Grofman, Handley, and Niemi 1992, pp. 107—8; Grofman and Davidson 1992, pp. 206—8.

28. Parenti 1986, p. 220.

29. Ibid.

30. Goldenberg and Traugott 1984, p. 112.

31. Cohen 1963, p. 13.

32. Becker, Schwartz, and West 1984.

33. Such was the sentiment of Detroit mayor Coleman Young and his supporters.

34. Becker, Schwartz, and West 1984, pp. 28—29.

35. Ettema and Peer 1992; Reeves 1989; Traugott, Price, and Czilli 1993.

36. Ibid.

37. Jamieson 1992, p. 17.

38. Princeton political scientist Carol Swain is one such individual who holds this view. See Swain 1993, pp. 207—9. And for an insightful critique of Swain's work, see Kennedy 1993.

39. Pettigrew and Alston 1988, p. 32.

Chapter 2

1. Pettigrew and Alston 1988, p. 1.

2. Ibid.

3. See ibid.

4. Ibid., p. 16.

5. Balzar 1982.

6. Pettigrew and Alston, 1988, p. 17.

7. Ibid., p. 18.

8. Proposition 15—the "liberal" handgun-control ballot initiative—was the most touted nonracial explanation thought responsible for Bradley's razor-thin defeat. Pettigrew and Alston 1988, p. 30: "Many media analysts, searching for a nonracial explanation for Bradley's defeat, have seized upon the handgun-control vote. Propo-

sition 15, they argue, differentially attracted far-right voters to the polls, and once in the booth, they voted conservative across the board." Pettigrew and Alston challenge this conventional wisdom on several grounds. For additional empirical analysis of the effect of race on whites' voting behavior in the 1982 Bradley-Deukmejian gubernatorial contest, see Citrin, Green, and Sears 1990.

9. Kleppner 1985, p. 217.

10. Ibid.

11. Axelrod 1986.

12. Schuman, Steeh, and Bobo 1985, pp. 81–82. The survey questions asked repeatedly of white respondents during the past several decades are as follows: (1) "There's always much discussion about the qualifications of presidential candidates—their education, age, race, religion, and the like; if your party nominated a generally well qualified man for president who happened to be black, would you vote for him?" (Gallup); (2) "If your party nominated a black for president, would you vote for him if he were qualified for the job?" (National Opinion Research Center). First, although the wording of the Gallup and NORC black presidential survey items differ slightly, each makes a point of asking respondents only if they would cast a ballot for a qualified black candidate *nominated* by the respondent's own party. Second and perhaps most important, if election contests are about voters rendering a choice between *competing* candidates, one might inquire about the inferences drawn from such questions asked outside of an electoral context. Besides, absent parallel questions to control for survey response, it is not particularly clear which, if any, political candidates serve as points of reference to white respondents. Finally, as has been demonstrated in pre-election polls during numerous electoral contests involving black office-seekers, questions such as those by Gallup and NORC often lend themselves to social desirability bias. See, in particular, Finkel, Guterbock, and Borg 1991; Hatchett and Schuman 1975; Reeves 1994b; Traugott and Price 1991.

13. Campbell et al. 1966; Ranney 1962; Pettigrew and Alston 1988; Reeves and Cohodas 1995a.

14. Swain 1993, p. 209.

15. Reeves quoted in Cohodas 1994, p. 703.

16. See, for example, Grofman, Handley, and Niemi 1992, pp. 82–85.

17. Here I employ the specific term "social experiment," so as to draw a distinction between a classical laboratory experiment typically conducted in the natural and social sciences. See Babbie 1986; Kinder and Palfrey 1993.

18. Considering the limitations inherent in any single methodological approach and my inclination to surmount these weaknesses, I have combined elements of the public opinion survey and the laboratory experiment. Although survey and experimental studies are certainly powerful methods of investigation in their own right, used concurrently, they enable one to gain a much fuller description of the world—political or otherwise. For a more detailed discussion of this general point, see Iyengar and Kinder 1987; Kinder and Palfrey 1993.

19. The *New York Times* Metro edition was used for our content analysis.

20. Thernstrom 1987, p. 186.

21. Kinder and Palfrey 1993, p. 15.

22. Ibid., p. 23.

23. For specific details of the face-to-face public opinion survey, consult appendix B.

24. Schuman, Steeh, and Bobo 1985, p. 65: "There is substantial evidence that responses to many racial items are influenced by whether interviewers and respondents are of the same or different races. In the case of white respondents, in one controlled study the responses to a question on intermarriage varied by 46 percent depending upon whether the interviewers were white or black (Hatchett and Schuman 1975)." For this reason, when it was feasible, we indeed matched the race of the interviewer to the race of the respondent.

25. To assess the plausibility of the news articles' content and presentation, three pretests involving a total of 345 white individuals (327 undergraduate students and 18 adults) were conducted. The final articles sent to our study participants reflect the insight gained from these pretests. In addition, to increase the plausibility of the news story experiment, the content was meant to reflect particular aspects of the general reporting of print news coverage during the 1992 presidential campaign (i.e., town meetings) and a number of biracial election contests (most notably, the hotly contested 1990 North Carolina senatorial campaign between Republican incumbent Jesse Helms and his Democratic challenger, Harvey Gantt).

26. Kahn 1989.

27. See Sigelman and Welch 1991, p. 91 for a similar conclusion.

28. Iyengar and Kinder 1987, p. 13.

29. Kinder and Palfrey 1993, p. 5.

Chapter 3

1. Gans (1979: 79–80) suggests, for instance, that a number of theories underlie news selection: (1) the *journalist-centered* approach postulates that journalists largely determine what is deemed newsworthy; (2) the *organizational-centered* approach suggests that the structure of the news organization itself influences story selection; and (3) *factors outside the news organization* exert a significant influence on news selection. For other theories, see Epstein 1973; Hirsch 1977; Sigal 1973.

2. Again, this definition is provided by sociologist Paul Luebke. See Grofman, Handley, and Niemi 1992, pp. 106–7.

3. Content Analysis Study. *New York Times* (October 14, 1989): A27.

4. Content Analysis Study. *Seattle Times* (October 3, 1989): A1.

5. Content Analysis Study. *New York Times* (October 14, 1989): A27.

6. Content Analysis Study. *Seattle Times* (November 3, 1989): A1.

7. Parenti 1986, p. 220.

8. Content Analysis Study. *New York Times* (October 22, 1989): A1.

9. Content Analysis Study. *Seattle Times* (November 3, 1989): A1.

10. Despite leading in the first primary, Michaux lost to Tim Valentine, a white Democrat. During the general election campaign, however, Valentine did run political advertisements appealing to whites' racial fears and sentiments.

11. Bradley quoted in Pettigrew and Alston 1988, p. 67.

Chapter 4

1. See, for example, Schuman, Steeh, and Bobo 1985; Farley et al. 1994, pp. 763—67.

2. Fiss 1976, p. 152.

3. Farley et al. 1994, pp. 774—76.

4. Ibid.

5. Ibid.

6. Ibid.

7. See Kinder and Sears 1985.

8. An interesting discussion of this idea appears in Sigelman and Welch 1991, pp. 94—109.

9. Hacker 1995, p. 33.

10. See Sigelman and Welch 1991, pp. 94—109.

11. See Kinder and Mendelberg 1991.

12. Kleppner 1985, p. 63.

Chapter 5

1. Thernstrom 1987, p. 217.

2. Thernstrom quoted in Holmes 1996, Section 4, p. 1.

3. McLemore quoted in Cavanagh 1983, p. 4.

4. Pettigrew quoted in ibid., p. 28.

5. This survey question is a standard item used by the National Election Studies.

6. Citrin, Green, and Sears 1990, p. 76.

7. This standard survey item, known as the "trial heat" question, is used by a great many media organizations conducting polls to assess the relative standing of candidates vis-à-vis their opponents. See, for example, Lavrakas and Holley 1991.

8. I am especially indebted to Professor Gregory Markus of the University of Michigan for suggesting this interpretation.

9. Pettigrew quoted in Cavanagh 1983, pp. 28—29.

10. See, for instance, Kleppner 1985, pp. 250—51.

11. Pettigrew and Alston 1988, p. 11.

12. Iyengar and Kinder 1987, pp. 12−13.

13. Leslie McLemore quoted in Cavanagh 1983, p. 3.

Chapter 6

1. The comment is from historian and sociologist Chandler Davidson of Rice University. See Holmes 1996, Section 4, pp. 1−4.

2. Thernstrom 1987, p. 204.

3. Fields and Higginbotham 1996, p. 69. Moreover, the U.S. District Court acknowledged as much when it stated, "We in no way wish to understate the gravity of Louisiana's well-documented history of racial discrimination with regard to its voting policies." See *Hays v. Louisiana III*, U.S. District Court, Western District of Louisiana, Shreveport Division.

4. Engstrom et al. 1994.

5. Prestage and Williams 1982, p. 316.

6. Coleman 1996, p. A17.

7. See, for instance, Engstrom 1994; Guinier 1994; Guinier 1995; McDonald 1989.

8. Some critics have argued that majority-black election districts amount to guaranteed seats for blacks. I, however, do not believe this to be the case. Congressman Mel Watt of North Carolina, whose district is 53 percent black, perhaps said it best: "You don't take a 53 percent district and guarantee a black person they are going to get elected." Quoted in Cohodas 1994, p. 701.

9. Wardlaw 1994, p. B7.

10. Blacks constituted about 31 percent of Louisiana's population.

11. Barone and Ujifusa 1994, pp. 544−46; Duncan et al. 1996, pp. 560−61.

12. Mann 1992, p. xiii.

13. Thernstrom 1995, p. A15.

14. Swain 1993, p. 203.

15. *Shaw v. Reno,* 1993 (Justice O'Connor, delivering the opinion of the Court).

16. Ibid.

17. Ibid.

18. Ibid.

19. *Miller v. Johnson,* 1994 (Justice Kennedy, delivering the opinion of the Court).

20. Ibid.

21. The cases are *Bush v. Vera* and *Bush v. Lawson* (Texas) and *Hays v. Louisiana III.*

22. *Bush v. Vera,* 1996 (Justice O'Connor, delivering the opinion of the Court).

23. Ibid.

24. Lublin 1995, pp. 112−13.

25. Holmes 1996, Section 4, p. 1.

26. Pildes 1995, pp. C1, 4.

27. Duncan et al. 1996, p. 255.

28. Ibid. p. 1081.

29. Lublin 1995, pp. 112−13.

30. Hacker 1995, p. 232.

31. Farley et al. 1994, p. 757.

32. In 1994, Georgia representative Cynthia McKinney's district was 60 percent black. Newt Gingrich's Sixth Congressional District is 91 percent white. See Duncan et al. 1996, pp. 353, 365.

33. Fields and Higginbotham 1996, p. 69.

34. *Bush v. Lawson* (Justice Souter, dissenting).

35. Ibid.

36. Comments of Justice Antonin Scalia during oral arguments, December 5, 1995.

37. *Presley v. Etowah County v. Commission,* 112 Sup. Ct. 820 (1992).

38. Quoted in Davidson and Grofman 1994, p. 16.

39. Guinier 1995, p. 39.

40. Empirical evidence informs us that unless blacks constitute at least 40 percent of the population, a black office-seeker has less of a chance to get elected.

41. Richie 1994, p. A22.

42. Quoted in Cohodas 1994, p. 702.

43. Engstrom 1994, p. 687.

44. Richie 1994, p. A22.

45. Quoted in Cohodas 1994, p. 702.

46. Applebome 1994, p. E5.

47. See Carter 1994, pp. vii–xx.

48. Quoted in "Withdrawing Guinier Nomination" 1993, p. 1427.

49. Ibid., p. 1425.

50. *Bush v. Vera* (Justice O'Connor, delivering the opinion of the Court).

51. Thernstrom, for one, has made this argument.

52. *Bush v. Vera* (Justice Souter dissenting).

53. Sack 1996. Three black non-incumbent office-seekers competing in southern congressional races lost in 1996.

54. Garrett 1995.

55. Gates 1995, p. 68−69.

56. Ibid.

57. Du Bois 1911, pp. 62−64.

References

♦ ♦ ♦

Aberbach, Joel D., and Jack L. Walker. 1973. *Race in the City*. Boston: Little, Brown.

Abrams, Kathryn. 1988. "'Raising Politics Up': Minority Political Participation and Section 2 of the Voting Rights Act." *New York University Law Review* 63: 449–531.

Adams, William C. 1975. "Candidate Characteristics, Office of Election, and Voter Responses." *Experimental Study of Politics* 4: 77–88.

Allport, Gordon W. 1954. *The Nature of Prejudice*. Reading, Mass.: Addison-Wesley.

American National Election Studies, 1948–1994. CD-ROM. Ann Arbor, Mich.: Institute for Social Research.

Amy, Douglas J. 1993. *Real Choices/New Voices: The Case for Proportional Representation Elections in the United States*. New York: Columbia University Press.

Anderson, Barbara A., Brian D. Silver, and Paul R. Abramson. 1988. "The Effects of the Race of Interviewer on Race-Related Attitudes of Black Respondents in SRC/CPS National Election Studies." *Public Opinion* 52: 289–324.

Apostle, Richard A., Charles Y. Glock, Thomas Piazza, and Marijcan Suelzle. 1983. *The Anatomy of Racial Attitudes*. Berkeley: University of California Press.

Applebome, Peter. 1994. "Guinier Ideas, Once Seen as Odd, Now Get Serious Study." *New York Times* (April 3): E5.

Arterton, Christopher F. 1984. *Media Politics: The News Strategies of Presidential Campaigns*. Lexington, Mass.: Lexington Books.

Axelrod, Robert. 1986. "An Evolutionary Approach to Norms." *American Political Science Review* 80: 1095–1111.

Babbie, Earl. 1986. *The Practice of Social Research*, 4th ed. Belmont, Calif.: Wadsworth Publishing Co.

Ball, Howard, Dale Krane, and Thomas P. Lauth. 1982. *Compromised Compliance: Implementation of the Voting Rights Act*. Westport, Conn.: Greenwood Press.

Balzar, John. 1982. "Deukmejian's Denials," *San Francisco Chronicle* (November 4).

Barker, Lucius. 1987. "Ronald Reagan, Jesse Jackson, and the 1984 Presidential Election: The Continuing Dilemma of Race." In Michael Preston, Lenneal J. Henderson Jr., and Paul L. Puryear, eds., *The New Black Politics: The Search for Political Power*, 2d ed. New York: Longman.

Barnes, James A. 1990. "Minority Mapmaking." *National Journal* 22 (April 7): 837–39.

Barnett, Marguerite Ross. 1983. "The Strategic Debate over a Black Presidential Candidacy." *PS* 16: 489–91.

Barone, Michael, and Grant Ujifusa. 1994. *The Almanac of American Politics 1994*. Washington: National Journal.

Bartels, Larry M. 1988. *Presidential Elections and the Dynamics of Choice*. Princeton: Princeton University Press.

Bartley, Numan V., and Hugh D. Graham. 1978. *Southern Politics and the Second Reconstruction*. Baltimore: John Hopkins University Press.

Baxter, Sandra, and Marjorie Lansing. 1981. *Women and Politics: The Invisible Majority*. Ann Arbor: University of Michigan Press.

Becker, John F., and Eugene E. Heaton Jr. 1967. "The Election of Senator Edward W. Brooke." *Public Opinion Quarterly* 31: 346–58.

Becker, Lee B., Maxwell E. McCombs, and J. McLeod. 1975. "The Development of Political Cognitions." In Steven H. Chaffee, ed., *Political Communication: Issues and Strategies for Research*. Beverly Hills, Calif.: Sage Publications.

Becker, Lee B., Thomas A. Schwartz, and Sharon C. West. 1984. "A Report on Media Coverage of Magnum and Vista." Ohio State University, School of Journalism.

Belfrage, Sally. 1965. *Freedom Summer*. New York: Viking Press.

Bell, Derrick. 1987. *And We Are Not Saved: The Elusive Quest for Racial Justice*. New York: Basic Books.

———. 1992. *Faces at the Bottom of the Well: The Permanence of Racism*. New York: Basic Books.

Berelson, Bernard R., Paul F. Lazarsfeld, and William N. McPhee. 1954. *Voting: A Study of Opinion Formation in a Presidential Campaign*. Chicago: University of Chicago Press.

Berke, Richard L. 1991a. "Redistricting Brings About Odd Alliance." *New York Times* (April 8): A1, A11.

———. 1991b. "G.O.P. Tries a Gambit with Voting Rights." *New York Times* (April 14): E5.

Berry, Jeffrey M. 1989. *The Interest Group Society*, 2d ed. Glenview, Ill.: Scott, Foresman.

Bidinotto, Robert J. 1988. "Getting Away with Murder." *Reader's Digest* (July): 57–63.

Binion, Gayle. 1979. "The Implementation of Section 5 of the 1965 Voting Rights Act: A Retrospective on the Role of the Courts." *Western Political Quarterly* 32: 154–73.

Black, Earl, and Merle Black. 1987. *Politics and Society in the South*. Cambridge: Harvard University Press.

Black, Merle. 1978. "Racial Composition of Congressional Districts and Support for Federal Voting Rights in the American South." *Social Science Quarterly* 59: 435–50.

Bobo, Lawrence, and Franklin D. Gilliam Jr. 1990. "Race, Sociopolitical Participation, and Black Empowerment." *American Political Science Review* 84: 377–93.

Bobo, Lawrence, and James R. Kluegel. 1993. "Opposition to Race Targeting: Self-Interest, Stratification Ideology, or Racial Attitudes?" *American Sociological Review* 58: 443–64.

Bobo, Lawrence, Camille L. Zubrinsky, James H. Johnson Jr., and Melvin L. Oliver. 1994. "Public Opinion before and after a Spring of Discontent." In Mark Baldassare, ed., *The Los Angeles Riots: Lessons for the Urban Future*. Boulder, Colo.: Westview.

Bohrnstedt, George. 1971. "Reliability and Validity Assessment in Attitude Measurement." In Gene Summers, ed., *Attitude Measurement*. Chicago: Rand McNally.

Brace, Kimball, Bernard Grofman, and Lisa Handley. 1987. "Does Redistricting Aimed to Help Blacks Necessarily Help Republicans?" *Journal of Politics* 49: 169–85.

Branch, Taylor. 1988. *Parting the Waters*. New York: Simon and Schuster.

Brischetto, Robert, David R. Richards, Chandler Davidson, and Bernard Grofman. 1994. "The View from the States—Texas." In Chandler Davidson and Bernard Grofman, eds., *Quiet Revolution in the South: The Impact of the Voting Rights Act, 1965–1990*. Princeton: Princeton University Press.

Broder, David S. 1995. "Court Decision Defies History." *Boston Globe* (July 6): 11.

Brown, Peter A. 1991. "Ms. Quota." *New Republic* (April 15): 18–19.

Brown, Rufus P., Dale Rodgers Marshall, and David H. Tabb. 1984. *Protest Is Not Enough: The Struggle of Blacks and Hispanics for Equality in Urban Politics*. Berkeley and Los Angeles: University of California Press.

Brownstein, Ronald. 1991. "Minority Quotas in Elections?" *Los Angeles Times* (August 28): A1.

Bullock, Charles S., III. 1982. "Inexact Science of Congressional Redistricting." *PS* 15 (Summer): 431–38.

———. 1984. "Racial Crossover Voting and the Election of Black Officials." *Journal of Politics* 46: 238–51.

Butler, David, and Bruce Cain. 1992. *Congressional Districting: Comparative and Theoretical Perspectives*. New York: Macmillan.

Butler, Katharine Inglis. 1984. "Reapportionment, Courts, and the Voting Rights Act: A Resegregation of the Political Process?" *University of Colorado Law Review* 556: 1–97.

Button, James W. 1989. *Blacks and Social Change: Impact of the Civil Rights Movement in Southern Communities*. Princeton: Princeton University Press.

Cain, Bruce. 1992. "Voting Rights and Democratic Theory: Toward a Color-Blind Society?" In Chandler Davidson and Bernard Grofman, eds., *Controversies in Minority Voting: The Voting Rights Act in Perspective*. Washington: Brookings Institution Press.

Campbell, Angus. 1971. *White Attitudes toward Black People*. Ann Arbor, Mich.: Institute for Social Research.

Campbell, Angus, Philip E. Converse, Warren E. Miller, and Donald E. Stokes. 1960. *The American Voter*. New York: Wiley.

————. 1966. *Elections and the Political Order*. New York: Wiley.

Campbell, Donald T., and Julian C. Stanley. 1963. *Experimental and Quasi-Experimental Designs for Research*. Chicago: Rand McNally.

Carmichael, Stokely, and Charles Hamilton. 1967. *Black Power*. New York: Vintage Books.

Carmines, Edward G., and James A. Stimson. 1989. *Issue Evolution: Race and the Transformation of American Politics*. Princeton: Princeton University Press.

Carter, Stephen L. 1994. Foreword to Lani Guinier, *The Tyranny of the Majority: Fundamental Fairness in Representative Democracy*. New York: Free Press.

Cavanagh, Thomas E., ed. 1983. *Race and Political Strategy*. Washington: Joint Center for Political Studies.

Chaffee, Steven H., ed. 1975. *Political Communication: Issues and Strategies for Research*. Beverly Hills, Calif.: Sage Publications.

Citrin, Jack, Donald Green, and David O. Sears. 1990. "White Reactions to Black Candidates: When Does Race Matter?" *Public Opinion Quarterly* 54: 74–96.

Cohen, Bernard. 1963. *The Press and Foreign Policy*. Princeton: Princeton University Press.

Cohodas, Nadine. 1984. "Strom Thurmond: New Votes, Old Views." *Congressional Quarterly Weekly Report* 42 (January 14): 70.

————. 1993. *Strom Thurmond and the Politics of Southern Change*. New York: Simon & Schuster.

————. 1994. "Electing Minorities." *Congressional Quarterly Researcher* 4 (August 14): 697–720.

Coker, J. Bradford. 1989. "Virginia: Deju vu." *Polling Report* (November 20): 1.

Coleman, William T., Jr. 1996. "Discrimination by Redistricting . . ." *Washington Post* (March 25): A17.

Commission on Civil Rights. 1961. *Commission on Civil Rights Report*, Book 1: Voting. Washington: Government Printing Office.

————. 1968. *Political Participation: A Study of Participation by Negroes in the Electoral and Political Processes in 10 Southern States since the Passage of the Voting Rights Act of 1965*. Washington: Government Printing Office.

————. 1975. *The Voting Rights Act: Ten Years After*. Washington: Government Printing Office.

————. 1976. *Using the Voting Rights Act: Ten Years After*. Washington: Government Printing Office.

————. 1981. *The Voting Rights Act: Unfulfilled Goals*. Washington: Government Printing Office.

Conover, Pamela Johnston, and Stanley Feldman. 1989. "Candidate Perception in an

Ambiguous World: Campaigns, Cues, and Influence Processes." *American Journal of Political Science* 33: 912–40.

Converse, Philip E. 1972. "Change in the American Electorate." In Angus Campbell and Philip E. Converse, eds., *The Human Meaning of Social Change*. New York: Russell Sage Foundation.

Converse, Philip E., and Michael W. Traugott. 1986. "Assessing the Accuracy of Polls and Surveys." *Science* 234: 1094–98.

Cook, Fay Lomax. 1979. *Who Should Be Helped?* Beverly Hills, Calif.: Sage Publications.

Cook, Thomas D., and Donald T. Campbell. 1979. *Quasi-Experimention: Design and Analysis Issues for Field Settings*. Chicago: Rand McNally.

Davidson, Chandler. 1992. "The Voting Rights Act: A Brief History." In Bernard Grofman and Chandler Davidson, eds., *Controversies in Minority Voting: The Voting Rights Act in Perspective*. Washington: Brookings Institution Press.

Davidson, Chandler, and Bernard Grofman, eds. 1994. *Quiet Revolution in the South: The Impact of the Voting Rights Act, 1965–1990*. Princeton: Princeton University Press.

Davidson, Chandler, and George Korbel. 1981. "At-Large Elections and Minority Group Representation: A Re-examination of Historical and Contemporary Evidence." *Journal of Politics* 43: 982–1005.

Defner, Armand. 1973. "Racial Discrimination and the Right to Vote." *Vanderbilt Law Review* 26: 523–84.

Dillman, Don A. 1978. *Mail and Telephone Surveys: The Total Design Method*. New York: Wiley.

Downs, Anthony. 1957. *An Economic Theory of Democracy*. New York: Harper.

Drew, Dan G., and David Weaver. 1990. "Media Attention, Media Exposure, and Media Effects." *Journalism Quarterly* 67: 740–48.

Du Bois, W. E. B. 1903. *The Souls of Black Folk*. New York: Vintage Books.

———. 1911. "Starvation and Prejudice." *The Crisis* (June 2): 62–64.

Duncan, Philip D., Christine C. Lawrence, and the Staff of Congressional Quarterly. 1996. *Politics in America 1996: The 104th Congress*. Washington: Congressional Quarterly Press.

Dyer, Edward. 1972. "Media Use and Electoral Choices: Some Political Consequences of Information Exposure." *Public Opinion Quarterly* 35: 544–53.

Edds, Margaret. 1987. *Free at Last: What Really Happened When Civil Rights Came to Southern Politics*. Bethesda, Md.: Adler and Adler.

Edsall, Thomas Byrne, with Mary D. Edsall. 1992. *Chain Reaction: The Impact of Race, Rights, and Taxes on American Politics*. New York: W. W. Norton.

Eldeman, Murray. 1967. *The Symbolic Uses of Politics*. Urbana: University of Illinois Press.

Engstrom, Richard L. 1994. "The Voting Rights Act: Disfranchisement, Dilution, and Alternative Election Systems." *PS* 4 (December): 685–88.

Engstrom, Richard L., Stanley A. Halpin Jr., Jean A. Hill, and Victoria M. Caridas-Butterworth. 1994. "The View from the States—Louisiana." In Chandler Davidson and Bernard Grofman, eds., *Quiet Revolution in the South: The Impact of the Voting Rights Act, 1965–1990*. Princeton: Princeton University Press.

Engstrom, Richard L., and Michael D. McDonald. 1981. "The Election of Blacks to City Councils: Clarifying the Impact of Electoral Arrangements on the Seats/ Population Relationship." *American Political Science Review* 75: 344–45.

———. 1985. "Quantitative Evidence in Vote Dilution Litigation: Political Participation and Polarized Voting." *Urban Lawyer* 17: 369–77.

Engstrom, Richard L., and John K. Wildgen. 1977. "Pruning Thorns from the Thicket: An Empirical Test of the Existence of Racial Gerrymandering." *Legislative Studies Quarterly* 2: 465–79.

Entman, Robert M. 1989. "How the Media Affect What People Think: An Information Processing Approach." *Journal of Politics* 51: 347–70.

Epstein, Edward J. 1973. *News from Nowhere*. New York: Vintage Books.

Erbring, Lutz, Edie N. Goldenberg, and Arthur H. Miller. 1980. "Front Page News and Real World Cues: A New Look at Agenda-Setting." *American Journal of Political Science* 24: 16–49.

Ettema, J. S., and L. Peer. 1992. "Polls, Race and the Horserace: Newspaper Coverage of the 1989 and 1991 Chicago Mayoral Primaries." Paper presented at the annual meeting of the Midwest Association for Public Opinion Research, Chicago.

Farah, Barbara G., and Ethel Klein. 1989. "Public Opinion Trends." In Gerald Pomper, ed., *The Election of 1988: Reports and Interpretations*. Chatham, N.J.: Chatham House.

Farley, Reynolds, and Walter Allen. 1987. *The Color Line and the Quality of Life in America*. New York: Russell Sage Publications.

Farley, Reynolds, Howard Schuman, Suzanne Bianchi, Diane Colasanto, and Shirley Hatchett. 1978. "Chocolate Cities, Vanilla Suburbs: Will the Trend toward Racially Separate Communities Continue?" *Social Science Research* 7: 319–44.

Farley, Reynolds, Charlotte Steeh, Tara Jackson, Maria Krysan, and Keith Reeves. 1993. "Continued Residential Segregation in Detroit: Chocolate Cities, Vanilla Suburbs Revisited." *Journal of Housing Research* 4: 1–38.

Farley, Reynolds, Charlotte Steeh, Maria Krysan, Tara Jackson, and Keith Reeves. 1994. "Stereotypes and Segregation: Neighborhoods in the Detroit Area." *American Journal of Sociology* 100: 750–80.

Feagin, Joe R. 1991. "The Continuing Significance of Race: Anti-Black Discrimination in Public Places." *American Sociological Review* 56: 101–16.

Feagin, Joe R., and Melvin P. Sikes. 1994. *Living with Racism: The Black Middle-Class Experience*. Boston: Beacon Press.

Feeney, Susan, and Steve McGonigle. 1994. "Voting Rights: The Next Generation." *Dallas Morning News* (August 14–): A1, A26–27.

Fields, Cleo, and A. Leon Higginbotham. 1996. "The Supreme Court's Rejection of Pluralism." *Boston Globe* (June 30): 69.

Fineman, Howard. 1995. "Race and Rage." *Newsweek* (April 3): 23–25.

Finkel, Steven E., Thomas M. Guterbock, and Marian J. Borg. 1991. "Race-of-Interviewer Effects in a Pre-election Poll." *Public Opinion Quarterly* 55: 313–30.

Firebaugh, Glenn, and Kenneth Davis. 1988. "Trends in Anti-Black Prejudice, 1972–1984: Region and Cohort Effects." *American Journal of Sociology* 94: 251–72.

Fiss, Owen. 1976. "Groups and the Equal Protection Clause." *Philosophy & Public Affairs* 5: 107–77.

Foner, Eric. 1988. *Reconstruction: America's Unfinished Revolution, 1863–1877*. New York: Harper and Row.

Franklin, John Hope, and Alfred A. Moss Jr. 1994. *From Slavery to Freedom: A History of the African-Americans*, 7th ed. New York: McGraw-Hill.

Frederickson, George M. 1981. *White Supremacy: A Comparative Study in American and South African History*. New York: Oxford University Press.

Gamson, William A. 1992. *Talking Politics*. New York: Cambridge University Press.

Gans, Herbert J. 1979. *Deciding What's News*. New York: Random House.

Garrett, Robert T. 1995. "On Looking Beyond Race." Louisville (Kentucky) *Courier-Journal* (July 2).

Garrow, David J. 1978. *Protest at Selma: Martin Luther King, Jr., and the Voting Rights Act of 1965*. New Haven: Yale University Press.

Gates, Henry Louis, Jr. 1995. "Powell and the Black Elite." *New Yorker* (September 25): 64–80.

Goldenberg, Edie N., and Michael W. Traugott. 1984. *Campaigning for Congress*. Washington: Congressional Quarterly Press.

Goyder, John. 1985. "Face-to-Face Interviews and Mailed Questionnaires: The Net Difference in Response Rate." *Public Opinion Quarterly* 49: 234–52.

Graber, Doris A. 1984. *Processing the News*. New York: Longman.

Graham, Hugh Davis. 1990. *The Civil Rights Era: Origins and Development of National Policy, 1960–1972*. New York: Oxford University Press.

Greeley, Andrew M., and Paul B. Sheatsley. 1971. "Attitudes toward Racial Integration." *Scientific American* 225: 13–19.

Greenhouse, Linda. 1991. "Court, 6-3, Applies Voting Rights Act to Judicial Races." *New York Times* (June 21): A1.

———. 1995. "Court Hears Arguments on Race-Based Districts." *New York Times* (December 6): B11.

Grofman, Bernard, and Chandler Davidson. 1992. *Controversies in Minority Voting: The Voting Rights Act in Perspective*. Washington: Brookings Institution Press.

Grofman, Bernard, and Lisa Handley. 1989. "Black Representation: Making Sense of Electoral Geography at Different Levels of Government." *Legislative Studies Quarterly* 14: 265–79.

Grofman, Bernard, Lisa Handley, and Richard G. Niemi. 1992. *Minority Representation and the Quest for Voting Equality*. New York: Cambridge University Press.

Guinier, Lani. 1993. "Clinton Spoke the Truth on Race." *New York Times* (October 19): A29.

————. 1994. *The Tyranny of the Majority: Fundamental Fairness in Representative Democracy*. New York: Free Press.

————. 1995. "The Representation of Minority Interests." In Paul E. Peterson, ed., *Classifying by Race*. Princeton: Princeton University Press.

Hacker, Andrew. 1995. *Two Nations: Black, White Separate, Hostile, Unequal*. New York: Ballantine Books.

Hahn, Harlan, ed. 1972. *People and Politics in Urban Society*. Beverly Hills, Calif.: Sage Publications.

Hahn, Harlan, David Klingman, and Harry Pachon. 1976. "Cleavages, Coalitions, and the Black Candidate: The Los Angeles Mayoralty Elections of 1969 and 1973." *Western Political Quarterly* 29: 507–20.

Haider, Donald. 1989. "Race in the 1989 Mayoral Races." *Public Opinion Quarterly* 11: 16–18.

Hanushek, Eric, and John E. Jackson. 1977. *Statistical Methods for Social Scientists*. New York: Academic Press.

Harding, John, Harding Proshansky, Bernard Kutner, and Isidor Chein. 1969. "Prejudice and Ethnic Relations." In Gardner Lindzey and Elliot Aronson, eds., *The Handbook of Social Psychology, Volume 5*. Reading, Mass.: Addison-Wesley.

Hatchett, Shirley, and Howard Schuman. 1975. "White Respondents and Race-of-Interviewer Effects." *Public Opinion Quarterly* 39: 523–28.

Henry, Charles. 1987. "Racial Factors in the 1982 California Gubernatorial Campaign: Why Bradley Lost." In Michael Preston, Lenneal J. Henderson Jr., and Paul L. Puryear, eds., *The New Black Politics: The Search for Political Power*, 2d ed. New York: Longman.

Higginbotham, Leon A. 1996a. *Shades of Freedom*. New York: Oxford University Press.

————. 1996b. "The Hon. A. Leon Higginbotham's closing Argument in *Hays v. Louisiana*," *Lawyers' Committee for Civil Rights Under Law Committee Report*, Spring/Summer 1996, p. 23.

Higginbotham, Leon A., Gregory A. Clarick, and Marcella David. 1994. "*Shaw v. Reno*: A Mirage of Good Intentions with Devastating Racial Consequences." *Fordham Law Review* 62: 1593–1659.

Higginbotham, Leon A., and Aderson B. Francois. 1995. "The Supreme Court's Retrograde Ruling on Race." *Philadelphia Inquirer* (July 9): E5.

Hinckley, Barbara R. 1981. *Congressional Elections*. Washington: Congressional Quarterly Press.

Hirsch, Paul M. 1977. "Occupational, Organizational, and Institutional Models in Mass Media Research: Toward an Integrated Framework." In Paul M. Hirsch,

Peter V. Miller, and F. Gerald Kline, eds., *Strategies for Communication Research.* Beverly Hills, Calif.: Sage Publications.

Hirsch, Werner Z., ed. 1971. *Los Angeles: Viability and Prospects for Metropolitan Leadership.* Westport, Conn.: Praeger.

Holmes, Steven A. 1996. "But Will Whites Vote for a Black?" *New York Times* (June 16): Section 4, 1, 4.

Horowitz, Donald L. 1977. *The Courts and Social Policy.* Washington: Brookings Institution Press.

House of Representatives. 1981a. *Extension of the Voting Rights Act, Hearings before the Subcommittee on Civil and Constitutional Rights of the Committee on the Judiciary,* 97 Cong., 1st sess. Washington: Government Printing Office.

———. 1981b. *Voting Rights Act Extension.* H. Rept. 97-227, 97 Cong., 1st sess. Washington: Government Printing Office.

Hovland, Carl I. 1959. "Reconciling Conflicting Results Derived from Experimental and Survey Studies of Attitude Change." *American Psychologist* 14: 8–17.

Huckfeldt, Robert, and Carol Weitzel Kohfeld. 1989. *Race and the Decline of Class in American Politics.* Urbana: University of Illinois Press.

Hyman, Herbert H., and Paul B. Sheatsley. 1956. "Attitudes toward Desegregation." *Scientific American* 195: 35–39.

Irish, Marion. 1942. "The Southern One-Party System and National Politics." *Journal of Politics* 4: 80–94.

Iyengar, Shanto. 1979. "Television News and Issue Salience." *American Politics Quarterly* 7: 395–416.

Iyengar, Shanto, and Donald R. Kinder. 1987. *News That Matters: Television and American Public Opinion.* Chicago: University of Chicago Press.

Jackman, Mary R. 1978. "General and Applied Tolerance: Does Education Increase Commitment to Racial Integration?" *American Journal of Political Science* 22: 302–24.

Jackman, Mary R., and M. Crane. 1986. "Some of My Best Friends Are Black . . . : Interracial Friendship and Whites' Racial Attitudes." *Public Opinion Quarterly* 50: 459–86.

Jackson, Derrick Z. 1996. "The Supreme Court's Whitewash of Congressional Districts." *Boston Globe* (June 19): 15.

Jackson, Tara D. 1994. "Attitudinal Determinants of the Self-Reported Neighborhood Preferences of Whites and Blacks: Do They Help Widen the Racial Residential Segregation Gap?" Ph.D. diss., Department of Psychology, University of Michigan.

Jacobs, Paul W., II, and Timothy G. O'Rourke. 1986. "Racial Polarization in Vote Dilution Cases under Section 2 of the Voting Rights Act: The Impact of *Thornburg v. Gingles.*" *Journal of Law and Politics* 3: 295–353.

Jamieson, Kathleen Hall. 1992. *Dirty Politics: Deception, Distraction, and Democracy.* New York: Oxford University Press.

Jaynes, Gerald D., and Robin M. Williams, eds. 1989. *A Common Destiny: Blacks and American Society*. Washington: National Academy Press.

Johnson, Donald Bruce, ed. 1978. *National Party Platforms,* vol. 2, 1960–1976. Urbana: University of Illinois Press.

Joint Center for Political and Economic Studies. 1993. *Black Elected Officials: A National Roster,* 21st ed. Washington: Joint Center for Political and Economic Studies.

Joselyn, Richard. 1984. *Mass Media and Elections*. Boston: Addison-Wesley.

Judd, Charles M., and David A. Kenny. 1981. *Estimating the Effects of Social Interventions*. Cambridge: Cambridge University Press.

Jussim, Lee, Levita M. Coleman, and Lauren Lerch. 1987. "The Nature of Stereotypes: A Comparison and Integration of Three Theories." *Journal of Personality and Social Psychology* 52: 536–46.

Kahn, Kim F. 1989. "Does Being Male Help?: An Investigation of the Effect of Candidate Gender and Campaign Coverage on Evaluations of U.S. Senate Candidates." Ph.D. diss., Department of Political Science, University of Michigan.

Karlan, Pamela S., and Peyton McCrary. 1988. "Book Review: Without Fear and without Research: Abigail Thernstrom on the Voting Rights Act." *Journal of Law and Politics* 4: 751–77.

Katz, Phyllis A. 1976. "The Acquisition of Racial Attitudes in Children." In Phyllis A. Katz, ed., *Towards the Elimination of Racism*. Elmsford, N.Y.: Pergamon Press.

Kazee, Thomas. 1981. "Television Exposure and Attitude Change: The Impact of Political Interest." *Public Opinion Quarterly* 45: 507–18.

Kelley, Stanley, Jr., and Thad W. Mirer. 1974. "The Simple Act of Voting." *American Political Science Review* 68: 572–91.

Kennamer, Donald. 1987. "How Media Use during the Campaign Affects the Intention to Vote." *Journalism Quarterly* 64: 291–300.

Kennedy, Randall. 1993. "Blacks in Congress: Carol Swain's Critique." *Reconstruction* 2: 34–40.

Kennedy School of Government Case Study. 1990. "Jesse Helms v. Harvey Gantt: Race, Culture and Campaign Strategy in the 1990 Senate Battle." Harvard University.

Key, V. O., Jr. 1966. *The Responsible Electorate*. Cambridge: Harvard University Press.

Key, V. O., Jr., with Alexander Heard. 1949. *Southern Politics in State and Nation*. New York: Knopf.

Kinder, Donald R. 1986. "The Continuing American Dilemma: White Resistance to Racial Change 40 Years after Myrdal." *Journal of Social Issues* 42: 151–71.

Kinder, Donald R., and Tali Mendelberg. 1991. "Cracks in Apartheid?: Prejudice, Policy, and Racial Isolation in Contemporary American Politics." Paper presented at the annual meeting of the American Political Science Association, Washington, D.C.

Kinder, Donald R., Tali Mendelberg, Michael C. Dawson, Lynn M. Sanders, Steven J. Rosenstone, Jocelyn Sargent, and Cathy Cohen. 1989. "Race and the 1988

American Presidential Election." Paper presented at the annual meeting of the American Political Science Association, Atlanta, Georgia.

Kinder, Donald R., and Thomas R. Palfrey, eds. 1993. *Experimental Foundations of Political Science*. Ann Arbor: University of Michigan Press.

Kinder, Donald R., and Lynn M. Sanders. 1996. *Divided by Color: Racial Politics and Democratic Ideals*. Chicago: University of Chicago Press.

Kinder, Donald R., and David O. Sears. 1981. "Prejudice and Politics: Symbolic Racism versus Racial Threats to the Good Life." *Journal of Personality and Social Psychology* 40: 414–31.

———. 1985. "Public Opinion and Political Action." In Jeanne N. Knutson, ed., *Handbook of Social Psychology*. San Francisco: Jossey-Bass.

King, Martin Luther, Jr. 1964. *Why We Can't Wait*. New York: New American Library.

——— . 1967. *Where Do We Go from Here: Chaos or Community?* New York: Harper and Row.

Klapper, Joseph. 1960. *The Effects of Mass Communication*. Glencoe, Ill.: Free Press.

Kleppner, Paul. 1985. *Chicago Divided: The Making of a Black Mayor*. DeKalb: Northern Illinois University Press.

Kluger, Richard. 1975. *Simple Justice: The History of* Brown v. Board of Education *and Black America's Struggle for Equality*. New York: Vintage Books.

Krueger, Richard A. 1994. *Focus Groups: A Practical Guide for Applied Research*, 2d ed. Thousand Oaks, Calif.: Sage Publications.

Kuklinski, James H., and Norman L. Hurley. 1993. "Hearing the Messenger but Not the Message?: Cue-Taking on the Issue of Black Self-Reliance." Paper presented at Political Psychology Conference, Champaign, Illinois.

Kurtz, Michael L., and Morgan D. Peoples. 1990. *Earl K. Long: The Saga of Uncle Earl and Louisiana Politics*. Baton Rouge: Louisiana State University Press.

Kuzenski, John C., Charles S. Bullock III, and Ronald Keith Gaddie, eds. 1995. *David Duke and the Politics of Race in the South*. Nashville: Vanderbilt University Press.

Lake, Celinda C. 1989. "Racial Sensitivity in Polling." *Polling Report* (November 20): 3.

Latimer, Margaret. 1987. "The Floating Voter and the Media." *Journalism Quarterly* 64: 805–12.

Lave, Charles A., and James G. March. 1975. *An Introduction to Models in the Social Sciences*. New York: Harper and Row.

Lavrakas, Paul, and Jack Holley, eds. 1991. *Polling and Presidential Election Coverage*. Newberry Park, California: Sage Publications.

Lawson, Steven F. 1976. *Black Ballots: Voting Rights in the South, 1944–1969*. New York: Columbia University Press.

———. 1985. *In Pursuit of Power: Southern Blacks and Electoral Politics, 1965–1982*. New York: Columbia University Press.

Lazarsfeld, Paul F., Bernard R. Berelson, and Hazel Gaudet. 1968. *The People's Choice*, 3d ed. New York: Columbia University Press.

Levine, Charles H. 1974. *Racial Conflict and the American Mayor.* Lexington, Mass.: D.C. Heath.

Lublin, David I. 1994. "Gerrymander for Justice?: Racial Redistricting and Black and Latino Representation." Ph.D. diss., Department of Government, Harvard University.

————. 1995. "Race, Representation, and Redistricting." In Paul E. Peterson, ed., *Classifying by Race.* Princeton: Princeton University Press.

MacKuen, Michael B. 1981. "Social Communication and the Mass Policy Agenda." In Michael B. MacKuen and Steven L. Coombs, eds., *More Than News: Media Power in Public Affairs.* Beverly Hills, Calif.: Sage Publications.

Mann, Thomas E. 1992. Preface to Bernard Grofman, and Chandler Davidson, *Controversies in Minority Voting: The Voting Rights Act in Perspective.* Washington: Brookings Institution Press.

Markus, Gregory B., and Philip E. Converse. 1979. "A Dynamic Simultaneous Model of Electoral Choice." *American Political Science Review* 73: 1055–70.

Martin, D. L. 1991. "Racial Voting in 1990: Helms v. Gantt for U.S. Senator in North Carolina and Legislative Term Limitations in California." Paper presented to the annual meeting of the American Political Science Association, Washington, D.C.

Massey, Douglas S., and Nancy A. Denton. 1993. *American Apartheid: Segregation and the Making of the Underclass.* Cambridge: Harvard University Press.

Matlack, Carol. 1990. "Questioning Minority-Aid Software." *National Journal* 22 (June 23): 1540.

Maykovich, Minako K. 1975. "Correlates of Racial Prejudice." *Journal of Personality and Social Psychology* 32: 1014–20.

McCombs, Maxwell E., and Donald L. Shaw. 1972. "The Agenda-Setting Function of the Mass Media." *Public Opinion Quarterly* 36: 176–87.

McConahay, John R., Betty B. Hardee, and Valerie Batts. 1981. "Has Racism Declined in America?: It Depends on Who Is Asking and What Is Being Asked." *Journal of Conflict Resolution* 25: 563–79.

McDonald, Laughlin. 1989. "The Quiet Revolution in Minority Voting Rights." *Vanderbilt Law Review* 42: 1249–97.

Mendelberg, Tali. 1992. "The Politics of Racial Resentment." Paper presented at the annual meeting of the Midwestern Political Science Association, Chicago.

Metz, David Haywood, and Katherine Tate. 1995. "The Color of Urban Campaigns," In Paul E. Peterson, ed., *Classifiying by Race.* Princeton: Princeton University Press.

Middelton, Russell. 1976. "Regional Differences in Prejudice." *American Sociological Review* 41: 94–117.

Morin, Richard. 1995. "A Distorted Image of Minorities." *Washington Post* (October 8): A1, A26–27.

Morris, Aldon D. 1984. *The Origins of the Civil Rights Movement: Black Communities Organizing for Change.* New York: Free Press.

Myrdal, Gunnar. 1944. *An American Dilemma: The Negro Problem and Modern Democracy.* New York: Harper.

O'Gorman, Hubert J. 1975. "Pluralistic Ignorance and White Estimates of White Support for Racial Segregation." *Public Opinion Quarterly* 39: 313–30.

Orfield, Gary. 1988. "Separate Societies: Have the Kerner Warnings Come True?" In Fred R. Harris and Roger W. Wilkins, eds., *Quiet Riots: Race and Poverty in the United States.* New York: Pantheon Books.

Orfield, Gary, and Carole Ashkinaze. 1991. *The Closing Door: Conservative Policy and Black Opportunity.* Chicago: University of Chicago Press.

Parenti, Michael. 1986. *Inventing Reality: The Politics of the Mass Media.* New York: St. Martin's Press.

Parker, Frank R. 1990. *Black Votes Count: Political Empowerment in Mississippi after 1965.* Chapel Hill: University of North Carolina Press

Pedhazur, Elazar J. 1985. *Multiple Regression in Behavioral Research: Explanation and Prediction.* New York: Holt, Rinehart, and Winston.

Peterson, Paul E., ed. 1995. *Classifying by Race.* Princeton: Princeton University Press.

Pettigrew, Thomas F. 1972. "When a Black Candidate Runs for Mayor: Race and Voting Behavior." In Harlan Hahn, ed., *People and Politics in Urban Society.* Beverly Hills, Calif.: Sage Publications.

————. 1976. "Black Mayoralty Campaigns," In *Urban Governance and Minorities,* Herrington J. Bryce, ed. New York: Praeger.

Pettigrew, Thomas, and Denise A. Alston. 1988. *Tom Bradley's Campaign for Governor: The Dilemma of Race and Political Strategies.* Washington: Joint Center for Political Studies.

Phillips, Barbara Y. 1983. *How to Use Section 5 of the Voting Rights Act,* 3d ed. Washington: Joint Center for Political Studies.

Pildes, Richard H. 1995. "Paying a Price for Colorblindness." *Washington Post Weekly Review* (April 24–30): C1, 4.

Pildes, Richard H., and Richard G. Niemi. 1993. "Expressive Harms, 'Bizarre Districts,' and Voting Rights: Evaluating Election-District Appearances after *Shaw v. Reno.*" *Michigan Law Review* 92: 483–587.

Pinderhughes, Diane. 1987. *Race and Ethnicity in Chicago Politics.* Urbana: University of Illinois Press.

Pinkney, Alphonso. 1984. *The Myth of Black Progress.* New York: Cambridge University Press.

Prestage, Jewel L., and Carolyn Sue Williams. 1982. "Blacks in Louisiana Politics." In James Bolner, ed., *Louisiana Politics: Festival in a Labyrinth.* Baton Rouge: Louisiana State University Press.

Preston, Michael, Lenneal J. Henderson Jr., and Paul L. Puryear, eds. 1987. *The New Black Politics,* 2d ed. New York: Longman.

Quinley, Harold E., and Charles Y. Glock. 1979. *Anti-Semitism in America.* New York: Free Press.

Ranney, Austin. 1962. "The Utility and Limitations of Aggregate Data in the Study of Electoral Behavior." In Austin Ranney, ed., *Essays on the Behavioral Study of Politics.* Urbana: University of Illinois Press.

Reed, Adolph L., Jr. 1986. *The Jesse Jackson Phenomenon: The Crisis of Purpose in Afro-American Politics.* New Haven: Yale University Press.

Reeves, Keith. 1989. "The Framing of Race as a Codeword by the Print Media in the 1989 New York Mayoral Campaign." Unpublished paper.

——. 1994a. "How to Adjust for the Disadvantage Black Candidates Suffer." *New York Times* (June 5): Section 4, 16.

——. 1994b. "Race as a Determinant of White Vote Choice in Biracial Election Campaigns." Ph.D. diss., Department of Political Science, University of Michigan.

——. 1995a. "Book Review: What Are We Reading?" *Quarterly Black Review of Books* 3 (September/October): 26, 44.

——. 1995b. "Racial Prejudice and Race-Baiting Election Appeals in Louisiana Political Campaigns." Expert Witness Report, U.S. District Court, Western District of Louisiana, Shreveport Division.

——. "Prospects For Black Representation After *Miller v. Johnson,*" In David A. Bositis, ed., *A New Framework for Redistricting: The Propects for Minority Representation Post-Miller.* Forthcoming.

Reeves, Keith, and Nadine Cohodas. 1995a. "Prevalence of Racial Bloc Voting Can't Be Ignored." *Miami Herald* (April 23): C5.

——. 1995b. "A Black Face Turns Away White Votes." *Wall Street Journal* (May 3): A19.

Richie, Robert. 1994. "False Choice on Voting Rights." *New York Times* (March 1): A22.

Robinson, John P., and Philip R. Shaver. 1973. *Measures of Social Psychological Attitudes.* Ann Arbor, Mich.: Institute for Social Research.

Rose, Douglas, ed. 1992. *The Emergence of David Duke and the Politics of Race.* Chapel Hill: University of North Carolina Press.

Rosenstone, Steven J., and John Mark Hansen. 1993. *Mobilization, Participation, and Democracy in America.* New York: Macmillan.

Rubin, Richard L. 1981. *Press, Party, and Presidency.* New York: W. W. Norton.

Sack, Kevin. 1995. "Court Draws Georgia Map of Congressional Districts." *New York Times* (December 14): A22.

Salmore, Barbara G., and Stephen A. Salmore. 1989. *Candidates, Parties, and Campaigns: Electoral Politics in America.* Washington: Congressional Quarterly Press.

Schlesinger, Arthur M., Jr. 1991. *The Disuniting of America: Reflections on a Multicultural Society.* Knoxville: Whittle Direct Books.

Schuck, Peter H. 1987. "What Went Wrong with the Voting Rights Act." *Washington Monthly* 19 (November): 51–55.

Schuman, Howard, Charlotte Steeh, and Lawrence Bobo. 1985. *Racial Attitudes in America: Trends and Interpretations.* Cambridge: Harvard University Press.

Scott, W. A. 1955. "Reliability of Content Analysis: The Case of Nominal Scale Coding." *Public Opinion Quarterly*: 19: 321–25.

Sears, David O., and Donald R. Kinder. 1971. "Racial Tensions and Voting in Los Angeles." In W. Z. Hirsch, ed., *Los Angeles: Viability and Prospects for Metropolitan Leadership*. New York: Praeger.

Senate. 1982a. *Voting Rights Act, Hearings before the Subcommittee on the Constitution of the Committee on the Judiciary*, No. J-97-92, 97 Cong., 2d sess. Washington: Government Printing Office.

———. 1982b. *Voting Rights Act Extension, Report of the Committee on the Judiciary, United States Senate*. S. Rept. 97-417, 97 Cong., 2d sess. Washington: Government Printing Office.

Shapiro, Robert Y., and Harpreet Mahajan. 1986. "Gender Differences in Policy Preferences: A Summary of Trends from the 1960s to the 1980s." *Public Opinion Quarterly* 50: 42–61.

Sigal, Lee V. 1973. *Reporters and Officials: The Organization and Politics of Newsmaking*. Lexington, Mass.: D. C. Heath.

Sigelman, Lee, and Susan Welch. 1984. "Race, Gender, and Opinion toward Black and Female Presidential Candidates." *Public Opinion Quarterly* 48: 467–75.

———. 1991. *Black Americans' Views of Racial Inequality: The Dream Deferred*. New York: Cambridge University Press.

Simon, Herbert A. 1955. "A Behavioral Model of Rational Choice." *Quarterly Journal of Economics* 69: 99–118.

Skrentny, John David. 1996. *The Ironies of Affirmative Action: Politics, Culture, and Justice in America*. Chicago: University of Chicago Press.

Sleeper, Jim. 1990. *The Closet of Strangers: Liberalism and the Politics of Race in New York*. New York: W. W. Norton.

Smith, Robert C., and Joseph R. McCormick. 1976. "The Challenge of a Black Presidential Candidate." *New Directions* 11: 38–43.

Smothers, Ronald. 1994a. "Jackson Tours to Tell Blacks of New Threat." *New York Times* (June 5): A13.

———. 1994b. "Black District in Georgia Is Ruled Invalid." *New York Times* (September 13): A14.

Sniderman, Paul, and Thomas Piazza. 1993. *The Scar of Race*. Cambridge: Harvard University Press.

Stanley, Harold W. 1987. *Voter Mobilization and the Politics of Race: The South and Universal Suffrage, 1952–1984*. Westport, Conn.: Praeger.

Stanton, Robert. 1996. "Minority Districts: Justice for Some, Gerrymandering for Others." *Headway* (March): 10–11.

Steeh, Charlotte, and Howard Schuman. 1992. "Young White Adults: Did Racial Attitudes Change in the 1990s?" *American Journal of Sociology* 98: 340–67.

Stempel, Guido. 1985. "Gate-Keeping: The Mix of Topics and Selection of Stories." *Journalism Quarterly* 62: 791–96.

Swain, Carol M. 1993. *Black Faces, Black Interests: The Representation of African Americans in Congress.* Cambridge: Harvard University Press.

Tabachnick, Barbara, and Linda Fidell. 1989. *Using Multivariate Statistics,* 2d ed. New York: Harper and Row.

Tate, Katherine. 1993. *From Protest to Politics: The New Black Voters in American Elections.* Cambridge: Harvard University Press.

Taylor, D. Garth, Paul A. Sheatsley, and Andrew M. Greeley. 1978. "Attitudes toward Racial Integration." *Scientific American* 238: 42–51.

Terkildsen, Nayda. 1993. "When White Voters Evaluate Black Candidates: The Processing Implications of Candidate Skin Color, Prejudice, and Self-Monitoring." *American Journal of Political Science* 37: 1032–53.

Thernstrom, Abigail M. 1979. "The Odd Revolution of the Voting Rights Act." *Public Interest* no. 55 (Spring): 49–76.

———. 1987. *Whose Votes Count?: Affirmative Action and Minority Voting Rights.* Cambridge: Harvard University Press.

———. 1995. "Racial Gerrymanders Come Before the Court." *Wall Street Journal* (April 12): A15.

Tipton, Leonard, Roger D. Haney, and John Basehart. 1975. "Media Agenda Setting in City and State Election Campaigns." *Journalism Quarterly* 52: 15–22.

Traugott, Michael W. 1992. "The Impact of Media Polls on the Public." In Thomas Mann and Gary Orren, eds., *Media Polls in American Politics.* Washington; Brookings Institution Press.

Traugott, Michael W., and Vincent E. Price. 1991. "Exit Polls in the 1989 Virginia Gubernatorial Race: Where Did They Go Wrong?" *Public Opinion Quarterly* 56: 245–53.

Traugott, Michael W., Vincent E. Price, and Edward Czilli. 1993. "Polls Apart: Race, Polls, and Journalism in Mayoral and Gubernatorial Election Campaigns." Paper presented at the annual meeting of the Association for American Public Opinion, St. Charles, Ill.

Tuchman, Gaye. 1972. "Objectivity as Strategic Ritual: An Examination of Newsmen's Notions of Objectivity." *American Journal of Sociology* 77: 660–79.

Turner, Charles F., and Elizabeth Martin, eds. 1984. *Surveying Subjective Phenomena.* New York: Russell Sage Foundation.

Tversky, Amos, and Daniel Kahneman. 1981. "The Framing of Decisions and the Psychology of Choice." *Science* 211: 453–58.

U.S. Civil Rights Commission. 1977. *Statement on Affirmative Action.* Clearinghouse Pub. 54 (October).

———. 1981. *Affirmative Action in the 1980s: Dismantling the Process of Discrimination.* Clearinghouse Pub. 70 (November).

———. 1993. Personal communication (August).

U.S. National Advisory Committee on Civil Disorders. 1968. *Report of the National Advisory Committee on Civil Disorders.* Washington: Government Printing Office.

Walton, Hanes. 1985. *Invisible Politics: Black Political Behavior*. Albany: State University of New York Press.

Wardlaw, Jack. 1994. "Reshaping Voting Districts: The Horns of a Dilemma." *New Orleans Times-Picayune* (July 31): B7.

Weaver, David H., Doris A. Graber, Maxwell E. McCombs, and C. H. Eyal. 1981. *Media Agenda-Setting in a Presidential Election*. Westport: Conn.: Praeger.

Webb, Eugene J., Donald T. Campbell, Richard D. Schwartz, and Lee Sechrest. 1966. *Unobtrusive Measures*. Chicago: Rand McNally.

Weisberg, Herbert F., and Jerrold G. Rusk. 1970. "Dimensions of Candidate Evaluations." *American Political Science Review* 64: 1167–85.

Welch, Susan. 1990. "The Impact of At-Large Elections on the Representation of Blacks and Hispanics." *Journal of Politics* 52: 1050–76.

West, Cornel. 1993. *Race Matters*. Boston: Beacon Press.

Williams, Linda. 1989. "White/Black Perceptions of the Electability of Black Political Candidates." *National Political Science Review* 2: 45–64.

Wilson, William Julius. 1990. "Race-Neutral Programs and the Democratic Coalition." *American Prospect* 1 (Spring): 74–81.

Winkler, Robert L., and William L. Hays. 1975. *Statistics, Probability, Inference, and Decision*, 2d ed. New York: Holt, Rinehart, and Winston.

"Withdrawing Guinier Nomination a No-Win Situation for Clinton." 1993. *Congressional Quarterly Weekly Report*. (June 5): 1427.

Wolfinger, Raymond E. 1965. "The Development and Persistence of Ethnic Voting." *American Political Science Review* 59: 896–908.

Wolfinger, Raymond E., and Steven J. Rosenstone. 1980. *Who Votes?* New Haven: Yale University Press.

Woodward, C. Vann. 1974. *The Strange Career of Jim Crow*. New York: Oxford University Press.

Zarate, Michael, and Eliot Smith. 1990. "Person Categorization and Stereotyping." *Social Cognition* 8: 161–85.

Table of Cases

◆ ◆ ◆

Index

♦ ♦ ♦